Praise for *Erotic Defiance*

Courtney Bryant's *Erotic Defiance* offers a refreshingly clear case for the erotic serving as a source of Black women's moral agency and demonstrates the value of striving for the possibilities created in the flesh. The chapters present erotic defiance as acts of care, acts of sexual agency, and acts of protest that provide novel ways forward to those seeking wholeness, mutuality, and justice. Ultimately, Bryant's unique gift to readers is an expansion of the erotic beyond sensuality, making this text a significant resource that reconnects us to our bodily autonomy, self-determination, and innate divinity.

—Monique Moultrie, PhD, author of *Hidden Histories: Faith and Black Lesbian Leadership* and *Passionate and Pious: Religious Media and Black Women's Sexuality*

A song of love for Black women's flesh, *Erotic Defiance* mines the moral potential of Black women's embodied agency. Bryant skillfully posits Black women's bodily practices of loving care as mechanisms of power that reveal a defiant womanist sacramentality that collaborates with the Spirit of God in its opposition to a racist-patriarchal status quo. There is no doubt that *Erotic Defiance* propels the field forward. It is a must-read for anyone compelled by Christian theological studies and Black womanist religious inquiry.

—Eboni Marshall Turman, PhD, associate professor of theology and African American religion, Yale Divinity School

There are books you read for knowledge, and there are books that do more than convey knowledge; they move you—to joy, and to tears. Courtney Bryant's *Erotic Defiance* is the latter. Drawing from, and extending, the womanist theoethical tradition, this text offers the erotic as a spiritually empowering and liberative ethical force in the world. Seriously researched, passionately argued, and beautifully written, *Erotic Defiance* is a work of love—a love that you can feel on every page.

—Dr. Biko Mandela Gray, associate professor of religion, Syracuse University, and author of *Black Life Matter: Blackness, Religion, and the Subject*

EROTIC DEFIANCE

EROTIC DEFIANCE

Womanism, Freedom, and Resistance

Courtney Bryant

FORTRESS PRESS
MINNEAPOLIS

Library of Congress Control Number: 2023937153 (print)

Cover image: Everyday in every way I'm becoming more confident - stock photo
©PeopleImages | Getty Images

Cover design: Kristin Miller

Print ISBN: 978-1-5064-7869-2
eBook ISBN: 978-1-5064-7870-8

For Khloe, Khaila, Afia, and Nana, that they might know their power.

And for all the beautiful girls in every shade of brown. This book is for you that you may always be aware of the awesome power that resides in your flesh.

Contents

Acknowledgments

This book is the product of many moments, thoughts, conversations, and prayers. While it has been a labor of my own body, it was birthed through relationships I hold near and dear. Primarily it is a testimony to the God of my life who has gifted me with a mind that always questions and has made sure fleshy and spiritual love has followed me all the days of my life. For this I give thanks. Writing, preaching, and teaching of You has been my life's joy.

This work would not have been done without the constant support of my mother and father, Irving and Dorothy Bryant, who taught me God's love and self-love and the dignity of my body so I would aways be free. For this I offer deep gratitude. I am also indebted to mentors in the spirit, bell hooks, Toni Morison, Gloria Naylor, Katie Cannon, and Karen Baker Fletcher, Black women whose fiery pens have inspired, guided, and encouraged this project from its inception to its completion. It has been the power of your words about Black women, our circumstances, and the ethic of love we have moved in despite the horrors we have had to live through that have emboldened me to write in season and out of season. It is also out of the witness of Dorothy Seward, Marjorie and Nicola Osinloye, and Ruthella Lewis, women who lived for the glory of God and nurtured the gifts inside of me so that I would be equipped to answer my call.

I also extend a special thank you to family by blood and the family who chose me: To Irving Bryant Jr., Alexus Bryant, and John and Tarikah Evans for always believing in me. To the Reverend Donna Owusu Ansah, my sister, friend, colaborer in the ministry, and conversation and prayer partner, for all the ways you see me, love me, and inspire me to be better. To my brothers and sisters in ministry, Sanetta Ponton, Kimmie Boyd, Marcia Norfleet, Kiki Barnes, Darriel Harris, and Shaun Saunders, who hold me accountable and prop me up. For the friendship and support of Gregory Gates, Theresa and Henry Baker, Kristin Smith, and Jennifer and Jawanza Clark; I treasure the gifts you brought to my life.

I am grateful also for places of encounter like Bethesda Baptist Church, the site in which I first met the Holy Spirit and began in earnest my spiritual development. To my forever pastor, the Reverend Dr. Allen Paul Weaver Jr., for helping me understand my call and calling me daughter no matter how far out I swim from shore. Thank you also to All Angels Church, to Jarrett Kerbell, James Lawrence, John Schmidt, Elam Lantz, Tania Oro-Hahn, Dina, Bologa and Pam Wong, who remind me how important it is to reach beyond what is comfortable and the beautiful gifts of God that await.

I am indebted to my teachers: Emilie Townes, who is always there with a word of encouragement and a word of wisdom; Victor Anderson, whose unrelenting critique and passion for teaching has sharpened my philosophical and theological analysis; and the womanist brilliance of Phillis Sheppard and Stacey Floyd Thomas.

To my Vanderbilt family: my principal conversation partner, Yolanda Norton, whose razor-sharp analysis was a gift untold in our many conversations on eros, the Bible, and the many ways Black women have forged survival out of lack, thank you for the ways you hold space for my brain and my heart. Thank you also to the gifted minds of Leonard Curry and Kyle Brooks for taking my ideas seriously and keeping them crisp in my mind and on my tongue. To Chelsea Yarborough for your authenticity, encouragement, and prayers and Prisca Dorcas Mojica Rodríguez for the ways your defiance inspired me. Though we were not at Vanderbilt at the same time, a special thank you to Biko Mandela Gray. This project's ethical precision would not be what it is without the many phone calls and debates we shared. Thank you for always being ready for my philosophical questions and helping me wrestle with "dead white men," the flesh, and moral agency.

To my Manhattan College colleagues, with special thanks to Nefertiti Takla, who reviewed chapters and let me read prose out loud. Thank you for being my "amen corner." Special thanks also to the MC Religious Studies Department for their support as I worked on the project.

Thank you also to the creative and resourceful Lynne Westfield for your mentorship, friendship, and opportunities for learning and writing. To the Fund for Theological Exploration, the Lilly Foundation, and the Louisville Institute for supporting my doctoral work through my dissertation and Wabash Center for Teaching and Learning for helping me take these ideas into the classroom.

Finally, I want to thank Fortress Press and my editor Ryan Hemmer, who has been an invaluable resource to me during this process. It has been such a blessing to work with someone who has from day one understood that this book was much more than an academic project, but a labor of love.

I do not for a moment take for granted the various manifestations of love and therefore God wrapped in flesh in my life. If I have forgotten anyone in my community, charge it to my head and not my heart. All of you have been integral. Thank you all for the life, strength, and courage you have breathed into me so that this book could be more than ideas in my head, but words on pages to be shared.

Introduction

Much has been said about the danger of bodies and flesh in the Christian tradition; however, this book focuses on their power. From the beginning, human bodies are divinely approved, declared suitable and fitting for God's purposes and pleasure. It is in encounter with these bodies—a physical, material interaction—that the Bible says God sought, when visiting Adam and Eve in the cool of the day, in the garden of Eden (Gen 3:8). The Bible repeatedly attests to God's love for and intimate cooperation with the bodies of God's children throughout history, detailing the critical role flesh holds in the manifestation of the divine in history. It is the bodies of Abraham, Puah, Moses, Rahab, John the Baptist, Mary, and others that God uses to prepare the way for Jesus, so that the Word might become flesh and right relationality between humanity and God would be restored and preserved.

Yes, flesh is important in the manifestation of God's will. Even the ways in which our corporeality is used in establishing covenants between God and humanity express the intimate nature of the relationship between our flesh and God. For example, the initial covenant between God and Israel is signified in the most intimate parts of men's bodies (circumcision) and the advent of salvation is materially accomplished through the most intimate part of a woman's body (vaginal birth). Moreover, the new covenant in Christ is predicated on the divinizing of flesh through the incarnation and the activity of human flesh as divine agent in the world, through the church. Bodies and flesh have always been key factors in the will of the divine. Yet, while we know of bodies as symbol and metaphor, little attention is given to the ways they build worlds.

This book at its heart is about our bodies and their capacity for the erotic—the manifestation of love in and through the flesh, the possibilities they produce, and how through our flesh we may be more deeply connected to God, ourselves, and others. Too often, Black women have yielded to Western

Christianity's anti-erotic culture, its misnaming of the erotic as evil, and most importantly its denial of the erotic's relationship to the divine. Rooted instead in the tradition of womanism, Black women's account of God, this book offers an alternative account of the erotic, positing it as a resource for Black women's moral agency.[1] Following in the tradition of feminist and womanist theology and ethics' account of the erotic as a divine, cohering, empowering, creative life force, I contend the erotic is the unifying force that makes collaboration between the Spirit and all flesh possible.[2] Moreover I argue the erotic restores the integrity of the relationship between body and being, drawing us deeper into relationship with God, ourselves, and each other. Present in the heightened awareness that comes with experiencing love and belovedness, like a mother cradling her child, an adult rubbing ointment on the back of their aging parent, or lovers in coitus, I aver the erotic is present in all love expressed with our bodies. This includes Jesus's body on the cross.

Through his incarnation we are reminded that our flesh is not only important to God, but God loves it and calls it home. Like Jesus, we too are temples of the living God, moving and breathing through God's presence within and through our acts of love, making God present in the world. Womanist M. Shawn Copeland writes that as the Christian moral exemplar, "Jesus of Nazareth is the measure or standard for our exercise of erotic power and freedom in the service of the reign of God and against empire."[3]

A key element of human dynamism, eros permeates spirituality, drawing our bodies and our being into deeper union with ourselves, the divine, and those with whom this energy is shared. This intersection is captured best

---

1 Womanism is an intellectual revolution in which Black women challenge "normative" white patriarchal epistemologies that marginalize and subjugate them and establish new epistemological, theological, and ethical methods and approaches based on their own experiences, in pursuit of their own actualization. Centering the real lives of Black women, womanist research methodologies privilege sources considered unorthodox. These include Black women's fiction, visual arts, fashion, music, religious rituals, and everyday practices of survival to provide a clearer vision of Black women's moral universes. For more, see Stacey Floyd-Thomas, *Mining the Motherlode: Methods in Womanist Ethics* (Cleveland: Pilgrim, 2006), xiii, 2–12.

2 In her treatment of Paul Tillich's reflection on eros, Keri Day contends eros actualizes agape and "as such love is manifested in and through the flesh." For more, see *Religious Resistance to Neoliberalism: Womanist and Black Feminist Perspectives* (New York: Palgrave Macmillian, 2016), 80.

3 M. Shawn Copeland, *Enfleshing Freedom: Body, Race and Being* (Fortress: Minneapolis, 2010), 65.

by Black culture's creatives, rather than traditional religionists, especially Black women writers, singers, and activists. African American poet Margaret Walker Alexander describes spirituality as "a consciousness of God's presence within us" and "being centered in a consciousness of divinity within all the time."[4] Suggesting a relationship between spirituality and sexuality, she argues that sexuality includes our spiritual selves, and that it is from both the spiritual and sexual aspects of Black women's existence that they create.[5] Alexander's connection between the spiritual and the sexual jives with womanist discourse on eros, and much of Black women's contemporary discourse on sexuality, yet we must be careful not to limit the connection between embodied love and spirituality to the sexual alone. As womanist theologian Karen Baker Fletcher contends, all acts of embodied love connect us to God within.[6] However, to embrace the erotic impulse, to seek after deep engagement with others, such that the boundaries of "what is appropriate" are blurred, or worse transgressed, is considered evil. To claim the connection between God and ourselves as erotic is blasphemous in normative Christian parlance. But to allow the erotic to authorize, such that alignment with one's authentic self becomes our moral guide, is perhaps the most transgressive of all—especially for Black women, whose bodies have been coded as sexual contagions of immorality, from which no good thing can come.

Western culture has deceived Black women about our bodies, their beauty, power, and possibilities, such that far too many of us are convinced that we are cursed, inferior, vile, and undesirable. As such, this project is a song of love, not only for Black women, but of love more generally and the ways love is manifested through flesh, especially Black women's flesh. It is predicated upon the notion that love makes possible humanity's access to the divine. Described by womanist theologian Karen Baker-Fletcher as the act through which body, spirit, and the divine connect, the act of loving is holy, and through acts of love, the body operates as an agent of the divine.[7] In the act of love, both loving and loved flesh encounter God, and in its wake life is

---

4 Dilla Buckner, "Spirituality, Sexuality and Creativity: A Conversation with Margaret Walker Alexander," in *My Soul Is a Witness: African American Women's Spirituality*, ed. Gloria Wade Gayles (Boston: Beacon Press, 1995), 224.

5 Buckner, "Spirituality, Sexuality and Creativity," 224.

6 Karen Baker-Fletcher, "The Erotic in Contemporary Black Women's Writings," in *Loving the Body: Black Religious Studies and the Erotic*, ed. Anthony Pinn and Dwight Hopkins (New York: Palgrave Macmillan, 2004), 203–4.

7 Baker-Fletcher, "The Erotic in Contemporary Black Women's Writings," 203–4.

affirmed, invigorated, and revitalized. For Baker-Fletcher, love manifested in and through the body is erotic, driven by eros, which she defines as a desire for union with the sacred.[8]

Like all bodies, Black women's bodies call attention to themselves through the senses: pain, fatigue, arousal, and a variety of hungers. According to Augustine and Aquinas, principal architects of what is understood as orthodox Christian theology, the body's hunger for pleasure beyond God's will is the primary obstacle to holy living and communion with God.[9] Consequently, the body maintains a complex and often contradictory position in the Christian theological tradition. For as dangerous as we have been told bodies and their corrupting desires are, they are also the material means by which humans seek, worship, and bear witness to the divine. Still, I am convinced that though many of us hold to the affirmation of the body as good, we are confused about its power.

While pleasure, as I argue, functions as an epistemology and is an important feature in identity formation and the impulse for resistance, I am fearful that sexual gratification has overdetermined our understanding of the erotic's power, mischaracterizing it to such a degree that we have forgotten how to seek fullness and fulfillment in other kinds of human relationality. This siloing of gratification and satisfaction is a dangerous tendency that causes many to go searching to fulfill yearnings for justice, connection, and wholeness in solely sexual ways, distracting us from the many modes of abundant living for which humans were created. Moreover, this siloing can hinder our participation in communal responsibility and accountability and the work of creativity in the world, which includes the construction of systems of mutuality and wholeness.

But how might a Black woman be whole in a world that denies that her moral agency is intelligible and meritorious? When the appearance of a self-possessed Black woman throws into upheaval the validity of white superiority and male sovereignty? When a Black woman's awareness of her divine right to self-authorize disrupts what imperialist, capitalistic white supremacy and

---

8 Baker-Fletcher, "The Erotic in Contemporary Black Women's Writings," 203–4.

9 Mark Barnes, "Thomas Aquinas on the Body and Bodily Passions," in *The Embrace of Eros: Bodies, Desires, and Sexuality in Christianity*, ed. Margaret D. Kamitsuka (Minneapolis: Fortress, 2010), 67. For more, see Augustine, *Confessions*, trans. Henry Chadwick (New York: Oxford University Press, 1991), bk. 2; and Augustine, *City of God*, trans. Marcus Dods, D.D. Book XIV (New York: Random House, 1950), bk. 16. For more on Aquinas's concept of human nature, see Eleonore Stump, *Aquinas* (New York: Routledge, 2003); and Thomas Aquinas, *Summa Theologia* I.75–76.

patriarchy call moral, traditional moral formulas cannot be trusted if Black women are to survive. In fact, Black women's survival demands that these formulas be defied. Defiance, as Katie Geneva Cannon argues, is the bedrock of Black women's moral agency.[10] Advancing Cannon's assertion, this book explores, expands, and promotes erotic defiance (a term I have coined) as a form of embodied agency fueled by the unctuous love of the physical and ontological being of Black women that invites the marginalized and the privileged alike to rebel against the assumed values and meanings of Black and female corporeality in the pursuit of the survival and flourishing of Black people, especially Black women.[11] This love is spiritual resistance. It is a form of embodied spiritual agency.

Though the phrase is my invention, erotic defiance is not new. It refers to a host of embodied practices that Black women employ to affirm the dignity and worth of Black and female corporeal being. By harnessing erotic power as a resource for moral good, erotic defiance asserts the notion of Blackness as desirable. It maintains a fierce love of and pleasure in Black flesh, offering an embodied praxis of self-definition and celebration that enables Black women to assert possession of their own bodies and resist social regulation, commodification, and degradation. Erotic defiance relies on both the symbolic and material aspects of the body to contest Black demoralization and combat the psychic and material obstacles it creates in the lives of Black people. Through bodily practices like touch, creativity, seduction, and protest, it asserts an individual's power for self-definition, self-authorization, and agency. Erotic defiance invites change in the moral universe by jettisoning the need for validation from the dominant culture. It embraces and even reveres that which dominant culture regards as inferior, dangerous, and depraved. It asserts the beauty, goodness, and truth of Black women, our bodies, and our being.

Through the language of ethics—what Black women do, particularly with our bodies—erotic defiance rejects and refutes Black women's status as objects of profit and pleasure for white society and asserts their own authority. In the spirit of James Cone's articulation of Black liberation, erotic defiance

---

10 Katie Cannon, *Black Womanist Ethics* (Eugene, OR: Wipf and Stock, 1988), 7, 104.

11 Katie Cannon borrows the term *unctuous* from writer Alice Walker. Unctuousness is a fortitude, determination, or courageous perseverance. But you do not arrive at unctuousness, according to Cannon; rather, Black women practice it in the negotiation of suffering, so not to be overwhelmed. Unctousness functions as counterbalance, "the interplay of contradictory opposites," the performance of love in an audience of detest. For more, see Cannon, *Black Womanist Ethics*, 92.

constitutes "the mind and body in motion—responding to the passion and the rhythm of divine revelation and affirming that no chain shall hold my humanity down."[12] Through these strategies and practices, Black women can reclaim their sense of personhood and ethical subjectivity, restore a positive relationship with their bodies, and cultivate a healthy concept of self. These practices have the power to create meaning, resignifying Black women's bodies and their erotic capacities as something to be honored, celebrated, and engaged. The result is the disruption, confrontation, interruption, and challenge of the racial hierarchies that create the oppressive circumstances of Black women and Black people as a whole.

Furthermore, it invites change in the moral universe by jettisoning the need for validation from the dominant culture. These practices have power. They create meaning, resignifying Black women's bodies and their erotic capacities as something to be honored, celebrated, and engaged. Practices of erotic defiance also yield disruption, confronting, interrupting and challenging the rationale of racial hierarchies that create the oppressive circumstances of Black women and Black people as a whole. So too, the liberation erotic defiance envisions is more than symbolic. It offers more than a counterargument to the ideology of Black inferiority and its notion that Black bodies exist for the profit and pleasure of whiteness and patriarchy. It portends the in-breaking of a new reality for Black women and their daily lives. By deploying the body in embodied acts of loving care for the sake of Black people collectively, erotic defiance enables Black women to confront and surmount the coercive authority of empire through the dynamic, relational, and signifying capacity of flesh. Through erotic defiance, Black women become change agents through collaboration with the Spirit of God.

While we have been socialized to believe that these miracles are restricted only to Christian bodies and Christian spaces, this book argues that both churched and unchurched bodies participate in creating new possibilities for Black women and the Black community through erotic acts. In other words, all kinds of Black women—from my indignant Nana and sanctified Mama, to my students and sister friends grappling with their relationships to God and religion—manifest God in flesh through embodied acts of love. No body is excluded from the possibilities of love. Not the beloved bodies of my sister friends who love other sisters, nor the bodies of those who sustain themselves

---

12 James Cone, *God of the Oppressed* (Maryknoll, NY: Orbis, 1997), 140.

through sexual service, like the bodies of church mothers and the bodies of ancestors like Fannie Lou and Ella Baker: all flesh possesses sacramental power. Often the site of the miraculous, Black female corporeality is indeed powerful, displayed as it spins hope out of despair and plenty out of scraps. Yet of all the powers it possesses, the greatest of these is love.

CHAPTER ONE

Bodies as Symbol, Flesh as Being

All of us, no matter what kind of body we possess, are captive, discursively and materially imprisoned by significations—the perceptions, interpretations, and value meanings—imposed upon us by a society that determines the limits of who we are allowed to be. The assembling of these meanings crystalize as a *signified* body, trapped in the symbolic order, carving out the boundaries of our being in a system of meanings, limits, and the practices they inspire. For a Black woman, the existential space afforded is narrow, far more so than the expansive boundaries of whiteness or maleness. Her body, marked by race and sex, restricts and even distorts her being. Governing her relationship with the world, it dictates how Black women are seen, interpreted, the freedom with which they can move, the power and status ascribed to their existence in a social world.

Violence has overdetermined Black female being. It has laid over, reconstructed, and disfigured Black femininity into a hypersexualized, debased monstrosity. The totalizing effect of this invention of the white moral imagination on the idea of Black womanhood and Black women's self-conception is best articulated in Nzotke Shange's play *For Colored Girls* when Juanita laments, "Ever since I realized there was someone called **a colored** girl, or an evil woman, a bitch, or a nag, I've been trying not to be that."[1] Black women do not recognize themselves in the hypersexual, beastly phantasm masquerading as Black womanhood. Eager to distance themselves from the significations imposed upon them, Black women often find themselves at war with their bodies. These distancing techniques take the form of denial of the flesh, the

---

1 Ntozake Shange, *For Colored Girls Who Have Considered Suicide When the Rainbow Is Enuf* (New York: Scribner, 2010), 56.

stifling of sexuality, sociality, and self-care such that the centers of pleasure, emotion, and pain are deadened to survive. Such survival, however, comes at a cost. It demands rupturing the sacred relationship between body and being, sacrificing one's wholeness and integrity, disintegrating the sacred union of spiritual and physical being. But if such sacrifices are necessary in order to survive the tripartite oppressions of racism, sexism, and classism, by what means can a Black woman be both whole and free in the material world?

Fragments of an answer begin to emerge as we investigate the practice of erotic defiance, an ethics of the body deployed by Black women throughout their history in the United States to assert their freedom. Erotic defiance leverages both the symbolic and material aspects of the body to contest Black demoralization and combat the psychic traumas and material obstacles they create in the lives of Black people. Through rituals of touch, self-making, and protest, erotic defiance asserts an individual's power for self-definition, self-authorization, and agency. But to better understand the mechanics of the practice, we must interpret them through "the haptic" and its power for the creation of meaning.[2]

The haptic is the power of the flesh to signify or create meaning through touch, through the relational capacities of the body and their impact on the world. From a theological lens it can be described as the corporeal facility that enables humans to cocreate with God. A discourse that exceeds spoken and written language, and articulates what Black feminist and literary critic Hortense Spillers calls a "grammar of black bodies,"[3] the haptic helps us to identify the relational capacity of bodies and underscore the often-discounted power of oppressed people. Drawing upon Spillers's account of "high crimes against the flesh" (the violent theft or the haptic dispossession of Black bodies that erodes and dislocates the Black self), I construct a womanist haptic analysis.[4] This analytic privileges the discursive role of the body, the physical

---

2 My use of the term *haptic* signifies the power of the body to affect the world and the world to affect the body. It is typically understood in theological scholarship as touch. For more, see Mark I. Wallace, "Early Christian Contempt for the Flesh and the Woman Who Loved Too Much in the Gospel of Luke," in Kamitsuka, *Embrace of Eros*, 33–49. Guided by film theorist Michelle Ann Stephans and phenomenologist Robert Sokolowski, I expand the category to include the haptic's multiplicity of physical, psychological, and social registers.

3 Hortense Spillers, "Mama's Baby, Papa's Maybe: An American Grammar Book," *Diacritics* 17, no. 2 (1987): 69.

4 Spillers, "Mama's Baby, Papa's Maybe," 67.

violence visited upon Black people, and its impact on the body's sociality (that is, what the body does, what has happened to the body, and how these elements contribute to identity, value meanings, and cultural procedures in the constitution of meaning). Haptic practices, the ways we relate physically or in embodied encounter, operate as a discourse, communicating the locus and position of Black existence in the social order, revealing the possibilities and limitations of Black identity and relationality.[5] Of particular import to this project is the ways encounters between subjects and the world engender alternative experiences that contribute to the construction of meaning in the individual and social imagination.

Through a close reading of Spillers's theory, I interrogate the distortion of Black female being through what I call the choreography of dispossession. The theft, violation, mutilation, and misappropriation of the Black body injure Black existence, fracturing Black consciousness and ontology as Black people as free beings are molded into abject objects.[6] An investigation into the haptic's role in the dis-integration of Black female being offers insight into the reach of the haptic and its power to disfigure not only Black bodies, but Black being. While the consequences of the haptic's power to alter Black being are grave, they also signal its potential as a curative strategy for the dehumanizing consequences of the construction of Black femaleness, concocted in an anti-Black moral imagination. Deploying Audre Lorde's theorization of the erotic, I consider the ethical implications of the haptic, constructing a moral paradigm in which the pornographic and the erotic serve as its defining poles. As one of the few resources of the oppressed that exists beyond the reach of racist patriarchy's distortion, I aver that the erotic—the capacity of the flesh to manifest and experience love—functions as the ethical apex of the haptic in Christian ethics. As such, I contend that the erotic capacities of Black female flesh are the wellspring by which Black women contest and escape the confines of an identity manufactured by whiteness, re-integrate dismembered aspects of their being, and articulate their freedom.

---

5 Haptic comes from the Greek *haptos*, which means "touch." The haptic is our bodily connectedness to the world and others. It includes bodily encounter, the impact and influence of our bodies on the world. This includes human practices, the activity of the body, and the engagement of the flesh by others. For more, see Wallace, "Early Christian Contempt for the Flesh," 33–50; and Michelle Ann Stephens, *Skin Acts: Race, Psychoanalysis, and the Black Male Performer* (Durham, NC: Duke University Press, 2014).

6 Spillers, "Mama's Baby, Papa's Maybe," 67.

BODIES MASQUERADING AS FLESH

In her canonical essay "Mama's Baby, Papa's Maybe," Hortense Spillers offers an account of the rupturing of Black female existence through the violent practices of chattel slavery's captivity and mutilation, such that the bodies of Black women become objects of white possession, vacant of a Black subject position.[7] Underscoring the atrocities visited upon Black female flesh—practices of seizure, abduction, containment, and degradation—Spillers chronicles the dispossession of Black corporeal autonomy or bodyright through the theft of the bodies of enslaved Africans, the severing of their motive will, and the resultant distortion of their sociality through their abject objecthood.[8] Spillers writes, "The massive demographic shifts, the violent formation of a modern African consciousness, that take place on the sub-Saharan Continent during the initiative strikes which open the Atlantic Slave Trade . . . interrupted hundreds of years of black African culture."[9] This "interruption" of Black African culture marks the ontological interruption of the Black self. For Spillers, flesh is "the primary narrative" of Black being, the mode of Black life incapable of alteration, the very substance of dignity, freedom, and relational possibility possessed by Black Africans, prior to their disfiguring encounter with Western man.[10] As a literary device, "flesh" represents the being that is obscured by the signified body—"the first creation," as philosopher of religion Charles Long describes it, created for freedom and relationship with God, unspoiled by domination.[11] Black flesh, Spillers contends, has a history of cultural practices, creativity, community, and a spiritual connection to the divine that spans centuries. Black nations created civilizations, practiced various forms of spirituality, built awe-inspiring architecture, and had complex economic and social relationships with neighboring countries and continents.[12] The imposition of the white gaze and white hands, however, interrupted the development of African identity, eclipsing it with its assumptions and deforming it with its expectations and exploitative demands.

---

7 Spillers, "Mama's Baby, Papa's Maybe," 67.

8 Christine Gudorf, *Body, Sex, and Pleasure: Reconstructing Christian Sexual Ethics* (New York: Routledge, 1995), 160.

9 Spillers, "Mama's Baby, Papa's Maybe," 69.

10 Spillers, "Mama's Baby, Papa's Maybe," 67.

11 Charles H. Long, *Significations: Signs, Symbols, and Images in the Interpretation of Religion* (Minneapolis: Fortress, 1986), 170.

12 Spillers, "Mama's Baby, Papa's Maybe," 67.

The distinction between "the body" and "flesh," Spillers writes, exists "between captive and liberated subject-positions."[13] The body, according to Spillers, is a theory. It has no physical properties. It is the product of hegemony's construction of Blackness, as well as practices and procedures of racism that escape discursive articulation. A prisoner of the symbolic order, the signified body exists as a phantasm of what womanist ethicist Emilie M. Townes describes as the fantastic hegemonic imagination, a world where ideology masquerades as history and truth.[14] This worldview maintains a reflexive relationship with the normative gaze, which inspires and regulates it, as it actively interprets all racial difference it encounters.[15] The meanings it assigns to the body are of great consequence. White institutional powers

---

13 Spillers, "Mama's Baby, Papa's Maybe," 67.

14 Emilie M. Townes, *Womanist Ethics and the Cultural Production of Evil* (New York: Palgrave Macmillan, 2006), 18. Townes argues the imagination is dangerously susceptible to hegemony—the ideology deployed by dominant groups to persuade the marginalized to docility. Consequently, stereotypes are embraced as truths. She writes, "Imagination is subordinated to the accepted moral landscape and its rules and sociopolitical and cultural realties." In this way, Townes joins the chorus of scholars who maintain that the realities of Black communities are regulated by hegemonic discourse, which casts Black people as caricatures of racist ideology.

15 Cornel West, "A Genealogy of Modern Racism," chap. 2 in *Prophesy Deliverance: An Afro American Revolutionary Christianity* (Louisville, KY: Westminster John Knox, 1982), 57. West, a religious philosopher, describes the normative gaze as the lens through which Western man orders and compares observations. The normative gaze is an ideal that privileges classical physical aesthetic values like light skin, blonde hair, and bodily and facial symmetry, as well as classical cultural standards, which include moderation, self-control, and harmony, prized in the Western imagination. As such those individuals who exhibited physical features most proximate to what they thought to be the Greco-Roman aesthetic ideal were perceived as the most beautiful and the most virtuous. As its discursive articulation, Enlightenment discourse was instrumental in codifying the normative gaze's negative designations of Blackness and establishing the Black body as a symbol of savagery, inferiority, and danger. Marked by an emphasis on empirical evidence, Enlightenment thinking fostered a preoccupation with what could be seen and what could be measured. Consequently what was visible, particularly physical appearance, was considered a reliable measurement of classification. Accordingly, Western notions of appropriateness and rationality mimicked the cultural standards of Greco-Roman culture. Enlightenment discourse formally established these discursive values of virtue, positioning African physical appearance and customs as the antithesis of whiteness, and alienated Black people from the category of humanness on the basis of physical characteristics, customs, and perceived intelligence, all interpreted through a Western lens. The normative gaze limits, caricaturizes, and misrepresents every body because representation as an epistemology—the act of basing one's knowledge on sight—leaves the world vulnerable to all sorts of interpretations, including the imposition of certain ideologies onto signs.

have repeatedly denied and castigated Black humanity and subjectivity, classifying Black people as limited or void of rational capacity or connection to God, prone to criminality and lasciviousness, and lacking moral fiber.[16] These caricatures confine Black identity to the boundaries of white imagination, calibrating society's engagement with actual Black flesh to conform to those boundaries. These meanings dictate how those of the dominant culture physically and materially relate to and treat those who are different. Despite its lack of literal mass, the signified Black body crushes Black being with the weight of fantasies of inferiority, immorality, and incomprehensibility. These imagined dangers sanction, and even encourage, violence for the sake of the safety, stability, and preservation of the sacred/natural orders of white society. It is to this Black body of significations, this static representation of true Black being, that the famous question "How does it feel to be a problem?" is posed.[17] However, Spillers's theorization of the flesh suggests that this "problem" is not the natural disposition of Black consciousness prior to white hegemony's distortion. Black flesh shares little in common with the signified Black body erected at the behest of whiteness. Black flesh means authentic Black material being, life, and the power that dwells within.

THE HAPTIC AS DISCOURSE

The literary functions of Spillers's theorizations of flesh and body become instructive in a discourse of the haptic. Representing Black life before its existential rupture and that which is left behind in its wake, the literary device of flesh offers a state of African being, unmolested before the dispossessing and distorting violence that reduces the Black self into a white abstraction and a mere object in a white world. In contrast, the signified body is a product of discursive power—the capacity of various modes of communication to regulate the epistemologies of the masses, to govern what we know and how we know it. It imbues certain people, places, cultures, and communities with value, while withholding or even robbing it from others.

Discursive power disempowers Black existence. It whittles the Black into a beast, riddled with uncontrollable sexual desire, stunted by intellectual and

---

16 Kelly Brown Douglas, *Stand Your Ground: Black Bodies and the Justice of God* (Maryknoll, NY: Orbis, 2015), 48–86.

17 W. E. B. Du Bois, *The Souls of Black Folk* (New York: Barnes & Noble, 2003), 8.

ontological inferiority, and contaminated by immorality.[18] Constructed as an oppositional identity to whiteness, this body of ideas creates a Black bogey(wo)man, an irrational monster, a sexually manipulative menace, a dimwitted sloth, and a litany of other inventions of white convenience to produce a false binary that designates whiteness as primary, central, normal, and valid, while Blackness is coded as subordinate, aberrant, inferior, and illegitimate.[19] From the words written and spoken about Black people, to Western media's visual depictions of Black people as criminals and prostitutes, to the invasion of hip hop culture by affluent white youth, Western modes of communication transmit, produce, and reinforce understandings of Black people, their significance and place in the social order, and the power given to or withheld from those who associate with them.[20] Shaping communal morality, discursive power calibrates the significance of right and wrong, determines proper conduct, and categorizes people for inclusion and exclusion, thereby governing the ethical dynamics of engagement, inclusion, and domination.

At the beginning of the twentieth century, discursive power's regulations demanded the separation of Black people from the wider public, which led to the state-sanctioned practice of segregation. The discursive Black body compelled the quarantining of the flesh of real Black people for fear of

---

18 For more, see Michel Foucault, *The Archaeology of Knowledge* (New York: Vintage, 1990), 17–35.

19 Black and womanist theologians and ethicists have also reflected on how the Black body, as carefully constructed symbol, is deployed by the dominant culture. Anthony Pinn emphasizes the importance of stylization in the significance of symbol and the Black body. He writes, "The black body isn't an image of society in the strict sense; rather the dehumanization of the black body promoted by the social system, is meant to maintain the system and reflect its wishes and fears." Arguing that the historic treatment of Black flesh is symbolically significant, he suggests that it is not just what is said about the Black body, but the violence visited upon the Black body that functions as a marker of white domination and the scandal of Blackness. Lynched Black bodies, or in its more contemporary iteration, Black bodies brutalized by police, serve to terrorize Black people and keep them ever mindful of the violent measures that will be taken in the maintenance of white supremacy and the containment of Black existence. Conversely, for those who subscribe to the ideology of white supremacy, particularly those threatened by Black prosperity, the murdered Black body as symbol represents the sovereignty of white power. For more, see Anthony Pinn, *Embodiment and the New Shape of Black Theological Thought* (New York: New York University Press, 2010); Kelly Brown Douglas, *Sexuality and the Black Church: A Womanist Perspective* (Maryknoll, NY: Orbis, 1999), 31–62; and Douglas, *What's Faith Got to Do with It? Black Bodies/Christian Souls* (Maryknoll, NY: Orbis, 2005), 109–49.

20 Douglas, *What's Faith Got to Do With It?*, 101.

contaminating the community with Black immorality. Black people were denied access to white schools, neighborhoods, and positions in white businesses and even white churches. Over half a century after the end of Jim Crow–era segregation laws, the same kinds of racialized logic and claims about the inferiority and danger of Black people continue to discursively operative in American life. And yet, the meaning of Blackness has not remained static. Instead it bends and twists in our communal imagination and brings in its torques and undulations the potential to transgress the rules of the signified body.[21]

The shifting meanings of Black embodiment point to the flexibility and malleability of meaning in the social world. Perpetually in flux, proper conduct and the basis for exclusion or inclusion differ based on the era and community in which discursive power operates. For example, the meanings, perceptions, and expectations of the Black signified body look dramatically different at a Klan rally in the early 1900s than at a Juneteenth cookout in Harlem in 2022. But the inclusion and exclusion discursive power hinges upon capitalize on the fundamental need of relational beings for recognition and belonging.

I felt the full weight of such exclusion firsthand, when I was removed from class in middle school and my mother was called into the principal's office. An intervention was deemed necessary because "I did not know my place." Twelve going on thirty-five, I had had the audacity to contest the narrative with which my health teacher was indoctrinating me and my classmates. She (and other teachers like her) was committed to reminding my classmates and me that the separate wing of the school that housed the coveted humanities program of which we were a part was intended to create physical and social distance between us and the contaminating influence of "those kids" not worthy of our exulted scholastic geography. The unspoken mantra of the program was "Be ye separate . . . and touch not the unclean thing," and it highlighted the

---

21 Pinn argues that Black bodies are not merely malleable symbols floating in the realms of written and artistic discourse, void of materiality. Black bodies communicate a language of their own. Pinn insists upon the social nature of embodiment: "Bodies . . . are . . . material realities that shape information within the context of the world." In effect, bodies also have an effect on the worlds they live in. Accordingly, the actual bodies of Black people inform, reflect, and resist the circumstances of oppression in the United States, highlighting the material body as a resource for moral agency. For more, see Pinn, *Embodiment and the New Shape*, xiii; Howard L. Harrod, *The Human Center: Moral Agency in the Social World* (Philadelphia: Fortress, 1981); and Copeland, introduction to *Enfleshing Freedom*.

dangers of intermixing.[22] The unclean thing, in this case, was students who were not part of the gifted and talented program—mainly students of color, whom these teachers never missed an opportunity to diminish.

Physically separated from the rest of the student population, this program limited our interactions with other students. The exposure we did get occurred as we passed through the halls for classes outside of the humanities program, during lunch, and the earful we received every time we went to health or art class.

Those kids aren't going anywhere. . . .
They're stupid and don't know how to act. . . .
They don't have what it takes to excel like yous do. . . .
You will see. The farther you stay away from them the better. . . .

Some of "those kids" were my friends; some were newer acquaintances; but all were students of color. While the academic space I spent most of my time in was racially mixed, after-school hours and weekends were spent with predominantly Black kids in my neighborhood, my church, and my living room. I had a brother who had attended the same school and hadn't had the opportunity to be a part of the humanities program. To hear my teachers tell it, he was going nowhere too.

While I didn't say much, my body language—my lack of eye contact, the lack of admiration, or perhaps the absence of the desire for approval from these women—erected a wall of hostility between them and me. One fateful day after getting my weekly lecture on the inferiority of "those kids," I could no longer hold my peace. I contested these women openly, out of respect for my friends and the many students who looked like me, but whose circumstances created obstacles that proved too overwhelming for them to participate in such programs. My teacher responded with gruffness, social demotion, and a negation of my presence whenever possible (with aspirations of soon taking steps to physically remove me from the program).

The discursive demonization of Blackness permeates the situation. From the disparaging words of my teacher, to the physical separation of Black students from "gifted" students in a separate wing, to the social shunning of the rebel student, unwilling to comply to the anti-Black worldview of

---

22 2 Cor 6:17 KJV.

her teachers, the choreography of the classroom communicated a system of values to those engaged in the debate, and instructed those who watched on passively. Everything, from the words they said to the consequences meted out for resistance, situated Black and white students alike in their appropriate location in the various economies of Western value.

The stakes of this conflict were far greater than I realized at twelve years old. My unwillingness to acquiese to my teacher's narrative was perceived as disrespect. I was challenging far more than her; I was challenging the prevailing beliefs of the social imagination. My unwillingness to affirm the values my health teacher was spouting, let alone participate in her moral universe, rendered me a problem. I too became a contaminating force that needed to be isolated, contained, removed, and warned against. Bucking the hegemonic discourse that secured her superiority, I stood in unapologetic solidarity with my Black peers. And that solidarity was read as offense, and as such I had to be disciplined—first by the teacher, then the institution, and hopefully, finally by my parents.

My transformation from promise to problem illustrates the ways discursive power translates to material power. It limits and constrains the movement of people with particular kinds of bodies and regulates where they can be and how they are required to act. These limits impact not only what Black people can do or where they can go, but their very identity. These dynamics often coerce Black folk into performances of docility, like that of the mammy, whose enthusiasm to wait upon white families, or the Uncle Tom, whose commitment to the preservation of white society to the detriment of himself, made them palatable to a white world and the white people who wielded such power in their lives. Such survival postures reify the performance of Blackness as subservience. While discursive modes of power are typically represented as spoken or written words, cultural theorist Stuart Hall emphasizes the elasticity of the concept of language. Hall concedes that "discourse is about the production of knowledge through language." But he insists that "since all social practices entail meaning and meanings shape and influence what we do—our conduct—all practices have a discursive aspect."[23]

My use of the haptic—the use and experience of the body's perceptive and relational apparatuses to construct meaning in the world—aims to amplify

---

23 Stuart Hall, "The Work of Representation," in *Representation: Cultural Practices and Signifying Practices*, 2nd. ed., ed. Stuart Hall, Jessica Evans, and Sean Nixon (Los Angeles: Sage, 2013).

the discursive nature of the haptic, particularly the way the handling of bodies communicates and alters the significance and status of embodied selves. Inspired by womanist theologian M. Shawn Copeland's and Hortense Spillers's use of the term as a linguistic device to account for the disfiguring of Black existence through the denigrating practices of chattel slavery, and Christian ethicist Mark Wallace's concept of haptology, or the theology of touch, my use of the haptic considers the theo-ethical implications of the treatment of Black women's bodies—their handling, the manner in which they are touched, or in the case of chattel slavery, abused, to investigate the way such practices impact Black women's performances of embodied moral agency.[24] Traditionally, haptology limits its scope to touch, however, womanist haptic discourse includes physical and nonphysical human practices of encounter, with special emphasis on the sociality of the body—the engagement of one's physical body by others and the power or effect of one's physical body on others and the world.

While the symbolic function of bodies as signs in the world is a key feature of the body's power, bodies are more than just signs. They are beings. Flesh and blood, they are living material agents that act and are acted upon. They touch and are touched, they relate and are related with, they affect and are affected. They signify. They create meaning. They substantiate and in some cases challenge the dominance of the spoken and written word, especially as it pertains to the discourse on Black corporeality. But the same principles that enable bodies to have an effect on their world make the body vulnerable to change as well. Felt not only on the body, the haptic registers on a "multiplicity of physical, psychological and social registers," according to film theorist Michelle Ann Stephens. Affirming the haptic's ability to form subjects, she writes, "The desire for difference is a fundamentally intersubjective formation

---

24 *Haptology*, a word religious scholar Mark I. Wallace coined for the theology of touch, accounts for the theological implications of the body's connectedness to the world and others, of bodily encounter, and of the impact and influence of our bodies on the world; this also informs my use of the haptic. This includes human practices, the activity of the body, and the engagement of the flesh by others. It also draws from film theorist Michelle Ann Stephens's sustained reflection on the haptic's multiplicity of physical, psychological, and social registers. Stephens's underscores at the figurative aspects of Black subjectivity's containment; however, the experience of subordination bears heavily on the material flesh, as well. Black flesh is disfigured by the hands that reject it, physically abuse it, dispossess it, disempower it, and spiritually desecrate it. These acts obstruct and limit Black women's bodily freedom to choose as it pertains to romantic partners, birth control, and pregnancy. The violence of erasure, subordination, and physical abuse communicates Black women's position in the world as one of no status, alienation, impotence, and contamination in ways linguistic modes of discourse do not.

felt on the body of the black subject as a touch. In other words, the black subject experiences symbolic capture in bodily sensational haptic terms."[25] Shared beliefs and standards experienced by the physical body in the form of containment assert the dominant community's distinction and communicate supremacy/inferiority through the manner certain bodies are handled and organized. In her book *Enfleshing Freedom*, Copeland underscores the haptic measures of chattel slavery's role in altering the identities of enslaved Blacks:

> The reduction and objectification of Blacks began with the seizure and binding of the body. The violent severing of the captive from community and personhood; imprisonment in dark and dank places below ground; packing and confinement in the slave ship. . . . More lessons in chattel slavery's idiom of power followed: handling and seasoning, bartering and selling.[26]

The handling of Black bodies, their seasoning, separating, torturing, and bartering, amplifies the impact of a multitude of haptic encounters in the deformation of the human status of African people in America.

As a result, these dehumanizing practices at the site of Black flesh initiate a kind of deformation in Black being. Through the haptic aspects of enslavement—transported, fed and bathed as animals, worked, whipped, and bred as something akin to a machine and a beast—enslaved Black people were denied human dignity and kinship relationships and robbed of their corporeal authority and autonomy, codifying their status and function as a commodity of whiteness. By usurping basic freedoms of humanity—whom to marry, whom to suckle, the bounds of free movement, when and how to work, when to rest, how to worship, and even the right to maintain familial and communal ties—slavery's haptic procedures governed Black existence and manipulated it into Black impotence. Though Black bodies remained, the Black subject was suppressed through humiliating, soul-murdering violence. Historian Nell Painter takes up soul murder in the lives of enslaved Blacks, describing it as a loss of self-esteem, depression, and anger.[27] However, she is not explicit about the role of such violence in dislocating the will and dispossessing the subject of its body.

Black humanist Anthony Pinn writes, "For blacks, social control and bodily control (or liberation) are oppositional and adversely related. The loss of control over black bodies (on a variety of levels) was a necessary component of

---

25 Stephens, *Skin Acts*, 21.

26 Copeland, *Enfleshing Freedom*, 29.

27 Nell Painter, *Soul Murder and Slavery* (Waco, TX: Markham Press Fund, 1995).

the social system, and structures were put in place to guarantee this loss of control."[28] Control over the image, agency, and labor of Black bodies is fundamental to America's economic livelihood, as well as the stability of the ideology of white supremacy, upon which its wealth is built.[29] Without it, American civilization and culture as we know it would cease to exist. Yet, ideology alone does not build civilizations. It is enacted by people, by flesh. Accordingly, the subordination of Black people in the United States has been carried out through physical and discursive violence upon their bodies, the very bodies by which America's fields were farmed and its national spaces were constructed.

By emphasizing bodies beyond their symbolic purpose, the haptic presents bodies as social and political actors that materially assert a reality that we can both see and experience. As such, in an increasingly political world, bodies are a primary site for realizing power. Black bodies are sites of contestation, the loci of warring racial ideologies, competing to claim both symbolic and material powers.[30] Consequently, bodily autonomy is a privilege these wars often usurp from Black people. In her work on victims of sexual assault, Christian ethicist Christine Gudorf defines bodyright as the ability to exercise control over one's body or personal autonomy.[31] Recognizing the body as the self, Gudorf argues that the "social recognition of bodyright is a prerequisite for full personhood and moral agency in humans."[32] Without this moral right, the very ability to be a moral agent is compromised.[33] Gudorf grounds her reflection on bodyright in the lives of sexual assault survivors and soldiers but gives little attention to those whose bodyright has been regularly withheld from them, Black men and women, and the impact it has on their moral agency. Gudorf's work is nonetheless instructive. Interpretations of the Black body and the parameters it imposes upon Black existence are oriented by doctrines of anti-Blackness that frame the discipling of Black people as a responsibility of white people and the bodies of Black people as a white possession secured by divine right. Even today, policies regarding women's reproductive rights and the enduring practices of police harassment and brutality testify to the

---

28 Anthony Pinn, *Terror and Triumph: The Nature of Black Religion* (Minneapolis: Fortress, 2003), 144.

29 For more, see Renee Harrison, *Black Hands, White House: Slave Labor and the Making of America* (Minneapolis: Fortress, 2021).

30 Pinn, *Terror and Triumph*, 144.

31 Gudorf, *Body, Sex, and Pleasure*, 160.

32 Gudorf, *Body, Sex, and Pleasure*, 161.

33 Gudorf, *Body, Sex, and Pleasure*, 161.

precarious status of the bodyright of Black people in America. Sovereignty over Black flesh, the ability to dominate, coerce, and discipline Black flesh, still functions as the principal marker of the glory of whiteness. On a macro level, Black people exist as the means of production to a white bourgeoisie, an underclass in contemporary American capitalism and a scapegoat for society's ills—violence, drug use, unemployment, and the shifting American morality. Rarely, however, do Black people enjoy that same freedom of bodily autonomy enjoyed by their white counterparts.

THE CHOREOGRAPHY OF DISPOSSESSION

The violent transgressions against Black women's bodies and bodyright include physical practices of seizure, containment, and exploitation. A choreography of dispossession maintains the authority, culture, and profit of every system of America from economy and entertainment to culture and politics. These haptic practices often confine and contain Black women physically and agentially in objectified modes of being that distort their humanity. The dehumanizing experience of powerlessness over one's body is also an assault on the African American soul. To describe these practices, I employ the language of choreography, a metaphor long utilized in womanist theological scholarship, to describe the dehumanizing acts of anti-Blackness and the strategic movement necessary for survival and transformation. On the pages of womanist scholarship, Black women are always dancing. Whether dancing reverently with God in spiritual kinship in the work of Karen Baker Fletcher; navigating systems of oppression in a dance that moves from the playful steps of the percolator to the protective stance of capoeira in the work of Emilie Townes; or twirling, lunging and leaping with Katie Cannon through the dance of redemption, courtesy of Bev Harrison, dance as a womanist metaphor for moral agency is not happenstance. It expresses the precarious state of Black women in an anti-Black world. Though they are adept in turning these steps into art, Black women's strategic movement is constant, as they are a target with a mark on their backs. While creative and innovative, these steps are nonetheless imperative for their survival, as they keep them moving, dodging, stymieing the aggression of empire.

As the deaths of Re'kia Boyd, Breonna Taylor, and Sandra Bland testify, the choreography of dispossession is the death-dealing dance of predator and prey. Black women are hunted, their flesh struck down in the violent ballet of white domination. But dispossession is not always so literal. Like the dance itself, the violence at its heart can also be symbolic; its death-dealing can take the form of social alienation, cultural suppression, and institutional coercion. Black female capture is often a symbolic and material demonstration of the consequences of Black women living beyond the boundaries of their prescribed place in a white world. Political activist and philosopher Angela Davis was targeted and imprisoned. Community organizer and speaker Fannie Lou Hamer was beaten and jailed. Journalist Ida B. Wells was harassed and exiled. In these cases, the containment of and violence against Black women aim to dispossess Black political and social agency to maintain white power in the society and politics. However, as the exploitation of Rosetta Tharpe, Sarah Bartmann, and every Black woman making 70 cents for every dollar a white man makes in 2022 indicates, the dance of disempowerment and distortion seeks also to exploit—to claim Black women's bodies, sexualities, labor, aesthetics, innovation, and industry as its own.[34]

The choreography of dispossession begins with the violent seizure of Black bodies from their native land and extends through the psychological and social disorientations such dislocation caused. Spillers and other historians have outlined the symphony of traumas visited upon Black enslaved people during the original abductions, but the disorientation of dislocation persists as a nagging reality of otherness and vulnerability in contemporary African American life as well. Far from their native land, the space Black women inhabit is traditionally caustic. Within a white-dominated society, Black women exist as demonized others. They are perceived as aberrations and their virtue is unintelligible to Western conventions of beauty and morality. Their dislocation heightens their vulnerability. While Black men and boys

---

34 Rosetta Tharpe was a singer and guitarist whose performance of her song "Hound Dog" was mimicked by Elvis Presley. While Presley became world renowned as the king of rock and roll, Tharpe remained in general obscurity, dying and coming to rest in an anonymous grave. For more, see Gayle Wald, "Reviving Rosetta Tharpe: Performance and Memory in the 21st Century," *Women & Performance: A Journal of Feminist Theory* 16, no. 1 (2006): 91–106. Sarah (Saartjie) Baartman was a Khosian woman from Africa whose physical prowess and large buttocks piqued the curiosity of the European gaze. With a promise of a career in performance and half of the profits, Sarah was swindled into slavery in England in 1810. For more, see Deborah Willis, *Black Venus 2010: They Called Her "Hottentot"* (Philadelphia: Temple University Press, 2010). For more information on the racialized gender pay gap, see Rakesh Kochhar, "The Enduring Grip of the Gender Pay Gap," Pew Research Center, March 1, 2023, https://www.pewresearch.org /social-trends/2023/03/01/the-enduring-grip-of-the-gender-pay-gap/.

are most frequently subjected to seizure by white authorities, the impact of the susceptibility of Black people to unmerited aggression, harassment, and bodily capture plagues the minds of Black women as well.

In her memoir, *When They Call You a Terrorist*, Patrisse Cullors recounts the ways her brothers were regularly rounded up in the streets and frisked by the LAPD, simply for being young, male, and Black. But even as a woman, Cullors was unable to sidestep the indignity of her brothers' seizure. Her gender did not allow her to evade the psychic and ethical implications of being powerless in the abuse of her loved ones. As she watched from the window, she too had to shoulder the trauma of these transgressions. She too had to submit to her own powerlessness against these injustices, knowing that at any moment she too could be snatched up for failing to perform obeisance to white authority. Cullors's inability to respond as a free, autonomous, and politically empowered being to the unjust humiliation of her brothers is reminiscent of countless stories in American life. In 2016, Diamond Reynolds, the girlfriend of Philando Castile, had to balance the tightrope of docility and advocacy as she negotiated with the police officer who shot her partner, while watching him bleed to death. The world watched as Reynolds patiently implored the officer to help her partner, as she broadcast from Facebook Live. Addressing the assailants with badges who shot Philando unprovoked as "Sir," Reynolds illustrates how Black women are forced to exercise unreasonable restraint and care as they judiciously choose their words in the midst of the horror of watching a loved one die before their very eyes.[35] These traumas and the social scripts that enforce and reinforce them rarely make headlines. There is not a day that goes by in America that some Black woman is not subjected to the trauma of violence against a loved one. As Spillers notes about these scenarios, though they are psychic victims themselves, Black women's lives are constantly swept under the brush of discourse as their identities are reduced to whatever role they served in the life of the primary victim.[36]

Black women, however, are not just bystanders in racialized extrajudicial violence. Sandra Bland's unnecessary arrest and subsequent death testifies to their direct vulnerability to seizure in contemporary America. Bland was on her way to a new job in Prairie View, Texas. After being stopped by a police

---

35 Yousur Al-Hlou, "Philando Castile, Diamond Reynolds and a Nightmare Caught on Video," *New York Times*, June 23, 2017, https://www.nytimes.com/video/us/100000005181340 /philando-castile-diamond-reynolds-and-a-nightmare-caught-on-video.html.

36 Spillers, "Mama's Baby, Papa's Maybe," 67.

officer for a minor traffic infraction—the failure to signal while she was changing lanes—Bland was manhandled by male police officer Brian Encina, because she failed to demonstrate the proper respect. After being slammed to the ground and mounted to be handcuffed, she was arrested and put in jail. Bland was later found hanged in her jail cell. Her death was ruled a suicide, a narrative her family contests to this day.[37]

The choreography of dispossession extends beyond bodyright to social freedom. The theft of Black women's bodies and their social status as chattel has had profound implications on their freedom of sociality—a quintessential aspect of personhood. The discursive and social procedures that render Black flesh contaminated degrades the sociality of Black life, manipulating it into new modes of embodied being. M. Shawn Copeland emphasizes the link between Black bodies as symbol and the historical status of Black people. She argues, "The body mediates our engagement with others, with the world and with the Other."[38] This mediation is facilitated by the symbolic meanings of bodies. She writes, "The social body's assignment of meaning and significance to race and/or gender and/or sexuality of physical bodies influences, perhaps even determines, the trajectories of concrete lives."[39] In other words, interpersonal engagements are calibrated by cultural perceptions of different types of bodies. Moreover, the predetermined perceptions of those bodies have institutional and structural ramifications, dictating how particular bodies will be treated, educated, and cared for, as well as the opportunities that will be provided for them. "The social body and physical body act on each other," Anthony Pinn writes, "the former attempting to define the possibilities of meaning and movement for the latter. They exchange meanings through a dialectic process of pressures and restrictions. In short, the social system seeks to determine the ways in which the physical body is perceived and used."[40]

Ineligible for recognition as humans, as social subjects, as ethical actors, Black people are relegated to the liminal space between subject and object. These deprecating encounters deny Black people the status of subjects, constraining their freedom to relate to others and to the world. As ethicist Stacey Floyd-Thomas has rightly argued, this demoralizing state of being destroys the

---

37 Gina Sunseri and Emily Shapiro, "Sandra Bland's Family Orders Independent Autopsy after Alleged Jail Suicide," ABC News, July 19, 2015, https://abcnews.go.com/US /sandra-blands-family-orders-independent-autopsy-jail-suicide/story?id=32552928.

38 Copeland, *Enfleshing Freedom*, 8.

39 Copeland, *Enfleshing Freedom*, 8.

40 Pinn, *Terror and Triumph*, 143.

ethical dimension of humanity—the ability to autonomously relate "between one human personality and another, between human personality and cultural institutions."[41] Attending to the subordination of Black women's subjectivity, Floyd-Thomas takes critical aim at celebrated social ethicist H. Richard Niebuhr's notion of the moral agency of the "responsible self," arguing, "Such agency is unavailable within the everyday reality of black women because she has neither the power, nor the social regard with which she can engage a man or God. Her experience of what it means to be human is thus denied."[42]

Recognizing the privilege/freedom of social relation as a mode of power, it becomes evident that the denial of Black people's power and autonomy to relate as human beings to the dominant culture and to each other inflicted great injury to Black existence and personhood. For example, W. E. B. Du Bois's discovery of his position in the social order was not discovered in a book, but through the experience of social rejection by a little girl, a newcomer to his childhood classroom, who refused to accept his Valentine's Day card.[43] He was slighted by this interpersonal encounter, and the rejection of Du Bois as suitable for friendly socialization in his elementary school classroom signaled to him his subordinate status, producing a psychological and social alienation that permeated every aspect of his life. Her rejection of him initiated "the shadow of the veil" in his life that swept over every aspect of Du Bois's social existence.[44] What is striking about this interaction is that it was executed by a child. She was most likely ignorant of the formal institutional, discursive constructions of Blackness that promulgated Black inferiority as the foundation of the authority of white supremacy. Yet, despite her youth, she was still attuned to the danger of relating with Du Bois, a Black boy, as her equal. She had already internalized a fear of the negative consequences such relating would have on her own social status as a privileged subject. The young woman's rejection illustrates the power of the haptic to communicate categories of social value and status assigned to Black flesh by the white gaze and thereby to obscure Black social being.

---

41 Spillers, "Mama's Baby, Papa's Maybe," 68.

42 Floyd-Thomas, *Mining the Motherlode*, xii.

43 Du Bois, *Souls of Black Folk*, 8. The veil signifies the social and psychological distance between the world Black people inhabit and their interiority. It also represents the distance between the white social world or white consciousness and the social world and interiority of Black people.

44 Du Bois, *Souls of Black Folk*, 8.

The distortion of Black female sociality and dispossession takes on a sexual dimension through the rape of Black women by white men, who seek to fulfill a libidinal desire for domination through the violation of Black women's physical being. With no legal protection from sexual violation or authority over their reproductive capacities, Black women during chattel slavery and beyond have existed in a state of sexual vulnerability that has influenced their choices regarding how they work, where they live, and even how they adorn and present themselves in larger society. For example, the urgency of developing new skills was a critical aspect of the Black Women's Club movement in the hopes of making Black women eligible for work beyond the domestic sphere and the reach of sexually violent white male employers. As historian Darlene Clark Hine explains, Black women's migration to the North at the turn of the twentieth century was an attempt to thwart white male Southerners, who believed no aspect of Black women's bodies were off limits and that as white men they were entitled to its pleasures. Even Clubwomen's emphasis on respectable attire was a strategy of dissemblance in the hopes that obscuring Black women's bodies from the gaze of white men might somehow safeguard them from sexual violence.

The violence of dispossession does not end with the bodies of Black women. It extends to the fruit of their wombs. Stolen from Black women (much like their bodies and their being), those born both out of loving unions and as a result of sexual violation were often sold for money, or as punishment for defiance. Modes of mothering took on the same dispossessive tone as other inhumanities of slavery. Acts of bonding, the experience of kinship, and even the cycles of life and death were withheld from Black women, as slave owners regularly practiced the cutting of family ties by separating mother from child, sister from brother, and loved one from loved one.[45] Described by Hortense Spillers as a state of kinlessness, the inability to mother the children that came from their wombs, maintain familial connections, or even choose a breeding partner was another means of eroding Black women's humanity and establishing their objecthood. With the 1807 prohibition of the importation of slaves, Black women's wombs became the exclusive soil from which Black labor was to be plucked. Essential to America's economy, the most sacred aspect of a Black woman's biology—her womb—was effaced as an instrument of industry. No longer a source of personal pleasure and creativity, her

---

45 Diana R. Berry, *The Price for Their Pound of Flesh: The Value of the Enslaved from Womb to Grave in the Building of a Nation* (Boston: Beacon, 2017), 10–32.

ability to generate more labor was commodified, motivating further sexual and reproductive dispossession as well as the erosion of her sexual freedom.

Long after the end of chattel slavery in America, the same logics of entitlement persist in the contemporary dispossession of Black women's bodyright. Bodily seizure morphs into bodily containment as the defilement of Black female bodyright by the dominant culture is mimicked by Black communities themselves. Especially prevalent in the Black church and even within Black families influenced by the controlling images of hegemony, many Black Christian communities demonize their women and exploit their bodies and labor to prop up Black patriarchal power. Both the Black church and the Black family operate as though Black women's bodies belong to the community. They demand that Black women offer their physical being in the service of the community's good, often at the expense of their own health and wholeness. As a result, as Chanequa Walker-Barnes argues in her book *Too Heavy a Yoke*, Black women become victims of cultural practices within their own communities that reduce their bodies to sexual objects and mechanize their creative capacity in collaboration with patriarchal traditions of women's subordination and service in general.[46]

While Black women fill the pews on Sundays, clean the building, prepare the food, teach the children, and fund the church with their tithes, a formidable contingent of the Black church (women included) vehemently rejects Black female leadership. While Black women have made huge strides in the professional arena, including representation on the Supreme Court, executive leadership of Fortune 500 companies, and status as the most educated demographic in America, those trends largely stop at the church door. In 2021, an AME congregation locked Rev. Ratona Stokes-Robinson out of the sanctuary, despite her being formally installed by the denomination's governing body. For weeks, Stokes-Robinson was forced to hold service in the parking lot of the church, because parishioners would not submit to female leadership.[47] Such stories are anything but rare, and indicative of the ways Black women's bodies are constrained from occupying spaces of authority and the way even Black communities enact the hostility of hegemony and the limitations of the

---

46 For more, see Walker-Barnes, *Too Heavy a Yoke: Black Women and The Burden of Strength* (Eugene, OR: Cascade, 2014).

47 Leonardo Blair, "Pastor Locked Out of AME Church by Members Due to Sex Finally Allowed Inside to Preach," Christian Post, November 3, 2021, https://www.christianpost .com/news/pastor-locked-out-of-church-due-to-sex-finally-allowed-inside-to -preach.html.

social imagination. The Supreme Court's recent ruling in *Dobbs v. Jackson Women's Health Organization* striking down the protections of *Roe v. Wade* offers another contemporary example of the dispossession of Black women's bodies. Though all women are affected by the ruling, Black women are disproportionately affected, as a footnote in the decision, written by Justice Samuel Alito notes: "A highly disproportionate percentage of fetuses aborted are black."[48] Additionally, Black women, many of whom disproportionately experience poverty, are less likely to have access to contraceptives and may not have the resources to travel to states whose abortion access remains intact. These circumstances further usurp Black women's bodily right to reproductive freedom and further complicate the lives of Black women in an already lacking and caustic environment.

The violence visited on the bodies of Black women bears heavy on Black female being like the burdensome "body of death" the biblical writer Paul implores God to be delivered from. While Paul contends Jesus will deliver the believer from this body of death, the Christian promise of freedom and liberation can only be experienced in the by and by, a world beyond time and space. Unwilling to delay freedom until death, Black women have attempted to create their own liberation in the here and now through a host of survival practices. Intended to help them elide pejorative narratives of Black womanhood and the violence those narratives invite, many Black women distance themselves from their bodies and the sexual designations assigned to them by suppressing the intimate parts of themselves—their sexuality, their emotions, and even the need for bodily self-care. Others have adopted the superwoman persona as a way of proving their worth and escaping assumptions of immorality. These patterns of disassociation from their bodily and emotional needs, intended as survival strategies, all to often contribute to further disintegration of their (Black female) subjectivity. In his essay "The Spirit Is Willing, but the Flesh Is Weak," practical theologian Lee H. Butler argues that Black people have historically operated in a mode of detachment, separating their spirits from their bodies to survive the psychic and physical violence of domination.[49] These coping strategies, he contends, reveal a level of self-inflicted dehumanization.

---

48 Anne Branigin and Samantha Chery, "Women of Color Will Be Most Impacted by the End of Roe, Experts Say," *Washington Post*, June 24, 2022, https://www.washingtonpost.com/nation/2022/06/24/women-of-color-end-of-roe/.

49 Lee H. Butler, "The Spirit Is Willing but the Flesh Is Weak," in Pinn and Hopkins, *Loving the Body*, 114.

Womanists like Katie Cannon contend this detachment manifests itself most readily in Black women's relationship with the erotic, and the intentional divorcing of spirituality from sexuality, which widens the fissure in Black female being and further injures Black women's ability to be relational beings. Exploring the existential conundrum Black women face as both sexual and spiritual beings, Cannon maintains that the religious and social formulations of virtue that elevate the spiritual/rational above the bodily lead Black women to sacrifice their sexualities for the sake of spiritual and social respectability.[50] These strategies represent the presence of rupture in the psyches of Black women, caused by significations of their bodies, cultivated by a social imagination mired in the values of white supremacy. Black women's selfhood thus becomes predicated on distancing themselves from the signified body and its sexual values by denying their physical bodies, desires, and needs in an attempt to disprove the myths promoted by white society. By performing acts of industriousness and value through service to their communities, their jobs, and their families (often at the expense of their own personhood), Black women themselves continue in the tradition of the erasure of their right to their own bodies and their own agency. Consequently, Black women often cannot escape a warped sense of their bodies and their erotic power, resulting in either silence and shame, or misconstrued versions of the erotic—the trope of sexual danger and combative sexuality.[51]

THE POSSIBILITIES OF THE FLESH

The significance of Black women's bodies in the white imagination and the violence it instigates facilitate Black women's ontological interruption. Epitomized by the disintegration of the body from a host of agential features (including dimensions of desire, will, and sociality), dispossessive violence and the strategies necessary for survival dislodge the will of Black female being, separating it from its corporeality, stifling the freedom and subjectivity of the self and transforming it into an object of exploitation. Of primary importance to this project is the way this disintegration discloses the malleable nature of existence

---

50 Katie Cannon, "Sexing Black Women: Liberation from the Prisonhouse of Anatomical Authority," in Pinn and Hopkins, *Loving the Body*, 12.

51 Combative sexuality is my own term. It signifies the use of one's sexuality as a weapon or tool for climbing in status through the exploitation of romantic and sexual partners.

and the body's role in the transformation of the self. In my own theological work, I've wrestled with the ontological significance of the physical properties of the body in Athanasius's *On the Incarnation* and placed it in conversation with Du Bois's literary metaphors of the flesh as veil, describing the flesh as "a portal of possibility and impossibility, becoming and interruption."[52] While Athanasius's theory of the flesh as veil provides access for Jesus Christ to heal humanity from the bondage of its fallen state, the Du Boisian veil of flesh obscures, separates, and interrupts. Du Bois describes the veil of his Black flesh, or Blackness, as an ever-present barrier that shuts out, stunting the capacities of personhood.

Similarly, Spillers illustrates the mangling of Black existence through the power of dispossessive domination in the West to dictate the nature of oppressed beings, such that Black people are confined in the meanings and limits decreed by the symbolic order. In this schema, one's physical embodiment and what happens physically to their body has the capacity to generate different states of being, from motherhood to kinlessness, from social and political actor to abject object. These dehumanizing atrocities register not only physically, but ontologically, mutating the function, capacities, and possibilities of Black being. Its existential parameters are altered such that all aspects of life—social, political, spiritual, psychological—suffer injury from procedures, postures, and practices that trample upon the bodyright of the selves subjected to such handling. While Athanasius, Du Bois, and Spillers each articulate the capacities of the state, status, and experience of the body to generate ontological change, Spillers's delineation of how violence alters Black ontology is perhaps most central to my argument.

While the malleable nature of the flesh—its vulnerability to undergo change—has left Black people depleted economically, socially, politically, and spiritually, that same plasticity serves as a sign of hope for liberation. The flexibility of the flesh suggests that the meaning of the body is always in flux and that haptic encounters will always produce shifts in identity, function, and significance. Moreover, flesh's flexibility discloses the liberative possibilities Black women as enfleshed agents can create through their corporeal impact on and in the world. Serving as the material and psychic substance of being, Black flesh mediates the desire and emotion of Black humanity and its relationship with the world and the other. Caught in their web of cultural expression, activism, and care, the Western world has been deeply impacted, transformed

---

52 Courtney Bryant, "Incarnational Power: The Queering of the Flesh and Redemption in Lovecraft Country," *Black Theology Journal* 19, no. 3 (2021): 207–17.

in thinking, inspired spiritually, and captivated by the presence and activity of Black women. These encounters, I argue, play an essential role in animating, communicating, and concretizing the significance of Black flesh assigned by white hegemony. But they have the power to challenge these significations too.

Spillers's distinction between the body and the flesh articulates the dramatic difference between a corporeal Black humanness, dignity, and freedom that live before and beyond the white gaze and Western man's invention of the Black body, its subordinate subjectivity, and its simulated meanings. So often in white culture the two are conflated, with the signified body masquerading as the identity and limit of Black life. Spillers's distinction discloses not only the substance of Black humanity—namely, a subject position equal to and capable of relating to the dominant culture—but also the captivating veneer of the Black body, laid over Black flesh, that imprisons Black humanity in abject objecthood, contorted and arranged at the will and pleasure of whiteness. This eclipse produces a perpetual stumbling block to the expression, freedom, and fulfillment of Black identity, fomenting rupture within the psyches of Black people, as they attempt to distance themselves from these impositions of identity. For white significations of Blackness mutate Black humanity's impulse. Rather than Black selfhood emerging from the organic desire, will, and emotion of Black people, it becomes a response to the myths of white society. Spillers's positing of the flesh as a malleable cultural artifact that holds cultural meanings through its various markings amplifies the haptic—the engagement of Black bodies and Black bodies' engagement with the world as a discourse by which the significance of Black bodies is constructed and communicated. It is to this discourse that we now turn.

Michel Foucault argues that power is reinforced through the institutional production and transmission of knowledge.[53] The haptic, I argue, discloses the power of the flesh of living beings to convey and reorganize meaning through its relationship with the world and other beings in the world. Despite the efforts of the West to produce a social system that rendered Black flesh abject objects devoid of ethical relationality, the haptic underscores the persistence of Black flesh and its indomitable relational dynamism. As the object and actor of the haptic—the ability to touch, to relate to, and to impact the other physically, spiritually, and mentally—the material body, the physical agent of the flesh is vital to Black liberation. Its influence on the imagination of others

---

53 Michel Foucault, *The History of Sexuality*, trans. Robert Hurley, vol. 1 (New York: Vintage, 1990), 100.

through experiences of encounter, or what phenomenologists call the sociality of the body, furnishes the technologies of signification—the ability to create meaning. Accordingly, flesh, as the conduit of physical relationality, has the power to shape and resist discursive constructions of objects in the world. This is particularly true of the flesh of those marginalized by race and sex, that is, Black women, given that the significations assigned to them are typically fabrications, produced and disseminated on behalf of racist patriarchy, that fail to reflect the reality of their beings. The contradiction between the identities invented by a social imagination warped by white supremacy and patriarchy and the realities of the oppressed demands that the flesh of Black women becomes the primary site of resistance. Consequently, the activity of material bodies—the physical manifestation of the flesh—and their impact on the imaginations of those who experience them ratifies, or challenges, the construction of the hegemonic imagination, particularly the effects of racialized and sexualized stigma on the people it degrades.

Haptic resistance to discursive formations disrupts the codification of the limits and values they impose and establishes an alternative reality. By imposing existential boundaries on its captives—who are typically poor and Black—discursive formation demarcates the boundaries of being and power permissible for the oppressed to occupy. Consequently, haptic sensations, which involve many senses simultaneously, extend beyond the physical to define the nature and limits of the character and freedom of Black people on psychic and social levels. More than simply touch, haptic sensibilities affect all aspects of the sensory experience of Black people, what phenomenologist Maurice Merleau-Ponty calls "their situatedness in the world."[54] For example, the Black body, harassed by police and incarcerated by the criminal justice system, and the Black community, overpoliced by law enforcement, experience the essential role haptic encounters play in animating and concretizing the significance of Black flesh as contemptible, faulty, and criminal.

Institutional knowledge disseminated through speech acts relies on the signifying power of the flesh's relationality, and in the case of conflict, the discourse of the body—those meaning-conveying acts—proves more powerful than words. This is in part because experience engages our tactile sense as a firsthand account, shaping what we understand to be true. Religion scholar Marleen de Witte argues, "Of all the senses, we take touch to be the one least

---

54 Maurice Merleau-Ponty, *Phenomenology of Perception*, trans. Colin Smith (London: Routledge and Kegan Paul, 1962), 137.

prone to trickery, the most direct of the senses, providing us with unmediated access to what—we presume—is real. More than seeing is believing, touching is believing."[55] For example, the 2023 shooting of Ralph Yarl, a sixteen-year-old who was shot for ringing the doorbell of the wrong house while trying to pick up his younger siblings, can be felt on more than the site of Ralph's gunshot injuries to the head and arm. They reverberate in the nervous systems of Black people who call the United States their home. The way the soul shudders and the skin crawls as we hear of incidents like this reinforces generations of fear and reinscribes the boundaries in which Black people are allowed to exist freely. The violence of one man on the body of one Black teen animates a legacy of containment and the inherent danger that accompanies being Black in America, regardless of any progress American politicians tout. In this way, the haptic provides sensory data that funds our sense of reality by reinforcing and actualizing value and significance through the material world and animating and concretizing the meaning of an object or subject.

If that which we can touch, see, and experience becomes our reality, guiding how we operate, flesh harnessed in particular kinds of religious and social praxis reveals the theoretical or ideological as mere conjecture. This is not to say that dismantling ideologies rhetorically is not an important aspect of resisting racist patriarchy, but that such strategies are incomplete until they are deployed materially. This is especially true as it pertains to assumptions about Black flesh. As Copeland and Spillers illustrate, the haptic was one of the primary technologies of the deformation of Black humanity. Thus, I maintain that interventions used to recover the humanity of Black people must include the haptic—fleshy practices that audaciously declare the power and subjectivity of Black people—as well. I aver erotic defiance—the willful embodiment of revolutionary and unapologetic love of, and pleasure in, the bodies and being of the oppressed—is such a practice.

MODALITIES OF THE HAPTIC:
THE PORNOGRAPHIC AND THE EROTIC

In her book *Enfleshing Freedom*, M. Shawn Copeland argues that the body is the means by which either the love of God or humanity's impulse of

---

55 Marleen de Witte, "Touch," *Material Religion: Journal of Objects, Art and Belief* 7, no. 1 (2011): 149.

domination is carried out.[56] The haptic, in my estimation, is the means by which Copeland's ethical modes of enfleshment and agency are executed. I contend that through the erotic, the body participates in the manifestation of divine transformative love, while the pursuit of domination through exploitation, as rehearsed in this chapter, can be classified as pornographic. The pornographic deploys the physical body, void of personal autonomy or under dysfunctional and exploitative interpersonal and intrapersonal relationality. Like Charles Carroll's project of religious racism that declared Black people void of a soul and therefore of connection to God, the pornographic seeks to sever the relationship between the divine and incarnated being.[57]

The Western project of the transubstantiation of Black flesh into objects to be owned, into things whose being was for their captors, is a pornographic process accomplished by dispossessing Black people of their bodies and thwarting the ethical relationality of Black flesh—its freedom, authority, and status. It relegates Black flesh to a pornographic embodied sociality that distorts Black humanity for the profit and pleasure (often sexual) of whiteness and white people, or as Audre Lorde explains "emphasizes sensation without feeling."[58] Made possible through the disconnection of one's body from their emotions, passions, desires, and the creative capacities constitutive of humanity, the rupture of body and being is in many ways a requirement of domination. These modes of existence produce and are products of violence. For example, the pornographic practice of breeding slaves, of slave masters coercing Black men to act as their proxy in the rape of Black women as they looked on, or the trauma of watching as offspring were gathered and sold, desecrates enslaved Black women's wombs and the human impulse for connection between mother and child. It also sows discord into the dynamics of

---

56 Copeland, *Enfleshing Freedom*, 1.

57 Writing in the late 1800s to early 1900s, Charles Carroll contributed to discourse that challenged the sacrality of Black humanity by arguing that Black people did not participate in the *imago Dei*—the image of God. While white humanity was connected to God through Adam and Eve, Carroll argued, Black people had no such connection. He writes, "Let us bear in mind that the Negro, the lower apes and quadrupeds all belong to 'one kind of flesh,' the flesh of the beast." Diminishing Black people to physical matter void of rational capacity or sacrality, Carroll's assertions demonstrate the role of Christian theology in validating racist oppression by advancing theories that Black people are divinely cursed and part of the order of beasts. For more, see Charles Carroll, *The Negro as Beast* (St. Louis: American Book and Bible House, 1900; repr., New York: Books for Libraries, 1980), 10, via Douglas, *What's Faith Got to Do with It?*, 130.

58 Carroll, *Negro as Beast*, 10, via Douglas, *What's Faith Got to Do with It?*, 130.

Black men and women's relationships. The indignity of experiencing bodily violation, particularly one's sexuality and reproductive capacities, and having no recourse to prevent it or protect oneself; the participation of Black men, whether coerced or not; and Black men's inability to protect Black women, Black children, or even themselves leave gaping relational scars and deep physical and psychic wounds carried by the flesh, but rarely uttered.

These obscene acts manipulate Black emotional sentience and disabuse Black flesh of its sacred intention, intending instead, as Audre Lorde argues, to suppress and exploit the life-giving power of authentic feeling.[59] The survival strategies of bodily estrangement Black women mount in response to the pornographic use of their flesh signals the creative facility pornographic practices can have on Black flesh. These acts do not generate life but instead silence the agent within, for like the torturous whip, they too tear bits of flesh, bits of Black humanness, away with every execution.[60] Bodily estrangement strategies testify to the ways those who experience oppression will often choose other forms of death, for the sake of relief from the ongoing spiritual agony of functioning as the refuse and undignified possession of the Western world.

In contrast to the pornographic, the erotic is a mode of relationality, powered by a divine force constitutive of humanness. Christian theologian Sarah Coakley asserts that given that eros is a manifestation of love, it is a manifestation of the divine. Building on Church Father Gregory of Nazianzus's metaphor of perichoresis,[61] she contends eros bears the *imago Dei* though its perichoretic operation. According to Gregory's metaphor, the Holy Spirit functions as a kiss, or desire enacted by the Father and received by the Son. Similarly, Coakley argues that the Holy Spirit demonstrates its erotic nature through its role of unifying the believer with God. She maintains that the indwelling of the Holy Spirit unites or coheres the believer to God and God to the believer, out of a desire for intimacy with each other.[62] Consequently, eros is a cause of coherence. It is the desire to know one another, to participate in

---

59 Audre Lorde, "Uses of the Erotic: The Erotic as Power," in *Sister Outsider: Essays and Speeches* (Berkeley, CA: Crossing, 1984), 54.

60 Spillers, "Mama's Baby, Papa's Maybe," 67.

61 Perichoresis signifies the divine dance between the three persons of the Godhead, the Father, the Son, and the Holy Spirit. Signifying the divine ethic of binding/cohering, the term *perichoresis* was originally used by church father Gregory of Nazianzus. For more on perichoresis, see Gregory of Nazianzus, *Epistle* CI, par. 4.

62 Sarah Coakley, *God, Sexuality, and the Self: An Essay 'On the Trinity'* (New York: Cambridge University Press, 2013), 49–50.

one another's lives, and to find home in each other. It animates deep engagement, not only with the bodies of the others, but the hearts, minds, and spirits of our human counterparts. In this way, eros/the erotic is a divine resource for moral agency.

Womanist theologian Kelly Brown Douglas insists that relationality calibrated by divine love is the intended aim of humanity. She writes, "A person's humanity is actualized when he or she, motivated by God's love, enters into a relationship with the rest of God's creation. To know the love of God is to be compelled to share that love with others. To do so is also to realize one's divinity."[63] Moreover, she writes that the *imago Dei* is reflected by men and women who choose to live in the world as "agents of loving relationship with God's creation."[64] It is the presence of God within humans and their willingness to exhibit the divine in loving relationality that constitutes humanness. This same presence and capacity for love bonds them to the divine. As such, participation in the dignity of others, despite the estrangement racial categorization creates, defies the alienating mechanisms of systemic evil and facilitates the intended purpose of humanity—to reflect and vivify the loving nature of God in creation.

But the erotic is not limited to expressing devotion to God through the love of one's neighbor. It extends to the experience of God through a deep and abiding understanding of self through love and pleasure that leads to more intentional living. "The measure between the beginnings of the self and the chaos of our strongest feelings," according to Lorde, "the erotic is an internal sense of satisfaction to which once we know it we can aspire."[65] The sensual is constituted by those physical, emotional, and psychic expressions of what is "deepest and richest within each of us."[66] Lorde locates the erotic between the origin of one's identity and the fullness of one's desire. Her repeated connection of the erotic to feelings and the sensual tethers the erotic to the body, for it is through the body that we experience the sensory. In this way, the erotic is a form of self-knowledge, a bodily way of knowing, making us aware of our capacity for joy and excellence.[67] It evokes a love, pride, and confidence in the wisdom of the body, the body itself as the arbiter of this

---

63 Douglas, *Sexuality and the Black Church*, 113.
64 Douglas, *Sexuality and the Black Church*, 114.
65 Lorde, "Uses of the Erotic," 54.
66 Lorde, "Uses of the Erotic," 54, 56.
67 Lorde, "Uses of the Erotic," 56–57.

knowledge and the truth of oneself, which it discovers as a result of sensory/ bodily pleasure. For some this awakening is aroused by sexual pleasure, for others the sensual, and still for others the spiritual, creative, or communal. Much of chapter 2 is dedicated to Black women's experience of the erotic as resuscitation. Made aware of their bodies' ability to enact and experience pleasure, they are changed, revived, and set free to more authentically live into the truth of themselves in much the same way the Holy Spirit gives new life.

Embedded deeply within us and inspiring our movements, the erotic functions on the level many religious communities describe as spiritual. However, for many Christians, likening the erotic to the spiritual constitutes blasphemy.[68] To mingle the sacred and the profane, or worse, to ascribe what is considered evil to God, seems too great a risk. But that which seems like conflict invites both philosophical and religious reconciliation. As Aristotle's philosophy of function insists, the function of a thing discloses its identity. From its effects, the philosopher can reason backward to actions, from actions to habits, from habits to powers, and from powers to identity. In an allied, metaphorical key, Jesus contends that one can know a tree by the fruit it bears.[69] The fruits of the erotic—affirmation, regeneration, empowerment— testify of its likeness to God. Consequently, the erotic is neither profane nor evil. It is a force, an emissary, or at the very least, a companion of the Spirit that bestows the life-inducing, healing, and empowering effects of the divine. Moreover, it is the erotic capacity of the flesh that connects it to the Spirit through the kinship between the spirit and the erotic.

The relational capacity of the flesh, operating in erotic modalities, functions agentially to resignify the Black body, particularly the defiant Black body, as something to be honored, celebrated, and related with, disrupting the racial hierarchies of hegemony, which dictate the oppressive circumstances of Black people. Black flesh in erotic celebration of itself and in pursuit of its own fulfill-ment (practices of erotic defiance) offers more than a counterargument to the

---

68 Historically, much of Christianity's discomfort with the body grows out of its deep suspicion of the erotic, also known as the passions. In Augustinian and Thomistic theologies, sexual desire is one of the markers that delineate the holy from the unholy. Commensurate with the ecclesial culture of their time, their theologies foster the notion that the presence of sexual desire connotes the absence of God and vice versa. For more on Christian erotophobia, see John E. Theil, "Augustine on Eros, Desire and Sexuality," in Kamitsuka, *Embrace of Eros*, 67–81.

69 Aristotle, *Nicomachean Ethics*, 2nd ed., trans. Terence Irwin (Indianapolis: Hackett, 1999), bk. 1:7, and Matt 7:16–20.

idea of Black inferiority and the notion that Black bodies exist for the profit and pleasure of whiteness. It offers an experience that can be participated in, the in-breaking of a new reality for Black women amid tyrannical systems of oppression. Through these practices, the body acts as the catalyst and locus of the in-breaking of material transformation.

In our contemporary moment, "the body," argues secular humanist Anthony Pinn, "affords an opportunity to challenge the dominance of the spoken and written word as the primary means of exchange."[70] With the advent of the digital revolution and the increasing popularity of video content, especially by the marginalized, the signifying power of Black flesh presents a grave threat to hegemonic epistemologies, while providing, through its ability to produce alternative knowledge, an arsenal of resources to Black moral agents who adopt its ethic of defiance. Uninterested in validation from the dominant culture and embracing, and even revering, the gifts that come from bodies deemed inferior, dangerous, and depraved, Black flesh through the power of the haptic disrupts oppressive constructions of Blackness through the revolutionary practice and performance of self-love. These practices offer a language of the body, operating at the haptic, as well as discursive, level through what I call erotic defiance.

Erotic defiance is resistance to the containment of Black flesh to the significations assigned to it by racist hegemony and the material bondage it facilitates. It is Black flesh stepping outside of the limits of its position as a possession of white culture, contesting racist ideology's invention of Black identity as false through the power of signification, a language of the body, "a language of ethics." I borrow this phrase from Penelope Ingram's *The Signifying Body*. Ingram argues for the relationship between ontology and ethics, contending that "being is revealed in and through an ethical relationship with the wholly other."[71] While I am unwilling to stake a claim on the distinct ontology of Blackness, if we consider ontology a way of articulating identity, her focus on the relational aspect of ethics as a source of disruption of false characterizations of Black people is generative. Following in the footsteps of Martin Heidegger, Ingram pushes past the representational function of language, which she believes is compromised by colonization, to posit a different approach to language that operates beyond metaphysics and relies on physical signification.[72] "This new

---

70 Pinn, *Embodiment and the New Shape*, 10.

71 Penelope Ingram, *The Signifying Body: Toward an Ethics of Sexual and Racial Difference* (Albany: State University of New York Press, 2008), xi.

72 Ingram, *The Signifying Body*, xi.

language is gestural, corporeal, and proximate," she argues.[73] Composed of the actions of the body, what we as people do in response to our encounter with others, this language discloses the authenticity of being. In this way, the experience of encounter becomes a new source of knowledge construction, provided by alternative experiences of the body, experiences that contradict dominant depictions of the marginalized other.

As much a part of the history of the politics of respectability as it is the politics of authority and refusal, erotic defiance represents Black flesh enacting a defiant love for itself, an independence of being, and an awareness of the importance of the material world to Black consciousness and moral agency. These tactics in their myriad of arrangements frustrate the perverse logic of racist ideology, which renders Black inferiority and corruption as static. This language of physical signification, which Ingram argues is ethics, reveals authentic being-in-the-world through ethical encounter with the other.[74] In agreement with Ingram I argue that as Black people engage in erotic defiance, as a language of ethics, it reveals an individual's authentic being in the world such that theoretically defiant postures refute the image of Blackness as static, demonstrating through the audaciously relational and resilient life of Black flesh that the significance of Black incarnated being is ever changing, growing, and becoming.

Ingram argues that these physical significations happen at the site of relational encounter. Bodies, in general, as objects in the world, have always functioned as living signs and symbols, which construct meaning through a corporeal language of signification. Operating at the level of the gaze, the culture of bodies is a prelingual language. It is the significance of bodies unmediated by words. Their arrangement, limits, and constraints; their inclusion and its criteria; their activity in the world; their interpersonal interactions: physical bodies in motion independently and interpersonally are didactic, offering insight into the relation of things in the world. It was these social queues, provided through the haptic culture of racial hierarchy, that offered unsolicited instruction to the white child who rejected Du Bois's valentine.

Kamala Harris's vice presidency and Ketanji Brown Jackson's recent ascendance to the Supreme Court offer contemporary examples of how the arrangement of bodies in cultural and political space contributes to the significance and status of bodies and the world. Vice President Harris's and Justice

---

73 Ingram, *The Signifying Body*, xi.
74 Ingram, *The Signifying Body*, xi.

Jackson's Black and female bodies inhabiting spaces of power alter societal notions about who can access power, what it means to be a political leader in America, and the significance of America as a nation, all while challenging the traditional limits of the Black female body. These Black women provide a kind of visibility/representation for the Black woman's body in spaces from which it had previously been excluded. Holding these offices alters notions of what is possible in the social imagination. In this way, despite Vice President Harris's hesitance to be a champion for policies specific to Black people, her presence as a Black woman advances the status and mobility of Black people on a representational level, transgressing the boundaries that previously seemed inviolable. From now on, the particularities of Black female embodiment are part of the nexus of practical and symbolic meanings and values assigned to American vice presidents and Supreme Court justices, and those meanings and values are part of the nexus of identity and action born along in and by Black women themselves. They expand the social imagination's horizon of possibilities when envisioning an American leader, while also adding to the horizon of possibilities when thinking of a Black woman.

The expansion and shifting of possible realities by bodies in motion are indicative of their capacity to be living signs and symbols that challenge discursive constructions. By demonstrating that what is deemed impossible based on racial ideologies is, in fact, possible, the power of bodies as living signs impacts the perspectives of those who are separated by racial difference, as well as those who share the same bodily classifications as Harris. As she is given entrée to political power, her presence broadens the realm of possibilities and obliterates limits imposed upon Black people, limits once operative in society. In addition, Kamala Harris's Black body is not only seen, but also experienced. Her ways and being contribute to intersubjective meaning on a larger level. As an ethical being involved in ethical relation with others, Harris, as vice president, relates to the whole country as one of its leaders. The experience of this relationship, whether on an intimate and personal level or on a macro, communal level, contributes to the perception, memories, imaginations, and choices that constitute the social imagination. The mode of relationality Harris executes, her decision to build or tear down, her practices, her choices, and even her gestures provide additional data to the project of the intersubjective construction of meaning.

Phenomenologist Howard L. Harrod's work is instructive here. Emphasizing the public nature of the life of the mind, and the social phenomenon of the life of reason, Harrod explains how actions, interactions, and the various activity of subjects in the world, the diversity of our "lives of reason," amalgamate and congeal into a common language of meaning and values, which coalesce at the sites of symbols and signs.[75] Accordingly, the nation's social imagination shifts as a result of its experience of having had a Black woman as vice president. Assumptions about race, once adopted as truth, suffer a crisis of legitimation when a Black woman takes the role of vice president, particularly one who is as intelligent, educated, eloquent, even-tempered, and composed as Harris. The application of traditional tropes about Black people being lazy, rationally deficient, incapable of self-control, and morally inferior are daily debunked. In this way, the experience of relating allows the perceptions of the other—that which is hidden or misrepresented in biased narratives—to be disclosed, and the shifting of perception, and therefore meaning, to occur.

Unfortunately, the lack of disruption Kamala Harris's presence offers on the political stage suggests that Black bodies even in spaces of power may be beholden to the terms of sociality established during chattel slavery, one limited to accessory and service to established structures of power. For Harris has been politically insignificant, suggesting that Western politics continues to exploit the bodies of Black women by obstructing any sightings of an insurgent Black political subject position. In other words, the dictates of political participation remain, and will remain until those given entrée into these spaces defy the political status quo, for bodies function not only as living signs that contribute to intersubjective meaning through their relational capacity, but also as material causes in the world. This too is rooted in the body's worldly activity. Bodies as living symbols that contribute to intersubjective meaning through the experience of ethical relation also inspire several practices. Surely a young Black woman with political aspirations sees Vice President Harris as a living symbol, bolstering her confidence that her dreams are within reach. Harris's actions and choices serve as a potential roadmap to potential success. However, glaringly absent is true resistance on the part of Black flesh that occupy these positions of power, communicating that the political mobility of Black flesh remains limited to particular performances of fealty to white power.

Political aspirants of all races may enact Harris's and Brown's corporeal and ethical postures as they reach for greater power and status, but the boundaries of acceptable behavior in order to attain these positions

---

75 Harrod, *Human Center*, 5.

will remain until there are enough successful examples of defiance to erect alternative possibilities in the minds of the social imagination. Time will tell if the presence of Black women in positions of leadership in America will move more of the next generation to enact defiance from within the political system than without. Still, for the young white woman or man who depends on the limitations of Black people to maintain their own status, Harris and Brown as living symbols can motivate violence, both in speech and practice, as a way to defuse the power of the corporeal symbol. For example, since Barak Obama's election as president, there has been great speculation as to whether the increase in racially motivated violence, from police officers shooting unarmed Black women and men to the election of Donald Trump, has been a form of backlash, inspired by the political achievement of a Black man and his inhabiting space and power intended only for white men. The reach of leaders like Representative Ayanna Pressley, journalist April Ryan, and Yamechi Alcindor offer a different narrative. These women have taken up postures of defiance to the status quo and have brazenly challenged the moral authority of political actors and parties hell-bent on oppressing Black people, people of color, and vulnerable populations. Each has gone toe-to-toe with presidents, the Republican and Democratic parties, and media outlets that peddle in misogynior to decry an unjust system, emboldening many from America's most oppressed communities to take up postures of defiance as well. Deploying defiance as a part of their political calling, these Black women have called new ways of thinking, being, and doing into being, and in so doing have expanded the confining space of Black women's existence

The haptic reach of the flesh—the way we use our bodies and their performances to impact the world, including our physical treatment of others; the way we use our corporeality to call things into being; that which we create; the environments and realities we conjure through the construction of new meanings—are immediate products of the physical body's power as a material cause. The power to shape, conjure, and create is facilitated by the cohering properties of the erotic. It is the use of one's erotic power—the power to draw, attract, and assemble energies and forces—that bring forth alternative realities in the world.

Black flesh holds divine power, the power to create as cocreators with God, and as M. Shawn Copeland argues, the power to manifest love on God's behalf. I contend that it is through the erotic that these bodies participate in the manifestation of God's love. Copeland tethers Black women's bodies to the divine through the *imago Dei*, which declares all of humanity is connected to God because it reflects God's image. Conceiving of the body as a human sacrament—a symbol of God's presence in concrete reality—Copeland suggests that Black women's affiliation with God and the ability of their bodies and personhoods to reflect the many manifestations of God's love, presence, rebuke, revelation, and the like oppose the conceptions of their existence funded by racist patriarchy.

The indomitable power of Black flesh is its haptic/relational capacity, which shapes and informs the world and the identity of the subject through its respective agential and sensory roles. The exercising of erotic modalities of the haptic (i.e., loving touch, celebratory and affirming cultural expression, and collaboration with the spirit of God on behalf of others) showcases the erotic's ability to repossess the bodies of Black women and to declare the sovereignty of God's order and God's intention of freedom. The free will of humanity is disclosed in our participation in the haptic. It is the capacity to produce goodness or evil in the world, through the power of the flesh and as such the physical manifestation of our moral agency. Producing goodness in the world, the erotic connects the self to the body, the divine, and others, allowing the manifestation of the love of God to orient the construction of knowledge and meaning in the world. Black women's deployment of erotic modalities of the haptic allows bodies to exceed their function as symbols, positioning them as sentient spiritual beings. Their feelings and desires become their own and the pleasure of wholeness and authenticity becomes their ethical guide. Enlivened by the erotic they operate in the resistance of erotic defiance, declaring the freedom and agency of Black women while frustrating the validity of racist patriarchy's misrepresentations of their moral and social status and its right to possess their bodies.

CHAPTER TWO

Erotic Resuscitation

The literary tradition of African American women curiously holds numerous depictions of Black women intimately handling one another's bodies in acts of bathing.[1] For the uninformed reader, these scenes register in the hypersexual key through which the Western world has trained its subjects to interpret Black women and their experiences. However, womanist ethicist Katie Cannon argues that embedded within the tradition lies the wisdom to properly interpret Black women's moral agency. More than mere fiction, Black women's literature is a key resource for understanding womanist ethics. It holds the values and attitudes Black women have adopted to maintain a posture of dignity, communicating, from one generation to the next, moral formulas for making a way out of no way, as racial domination and patriarchy wreak havoc on their lives.[2]

In keeping with this tradition, this chapter uses womanist moral theologian M. Shawn Copeland's theo-ethical analysis of the embodied ministry of Jesus and ethicist Marc I. Wallace's concept of haptology (the theology of touch) to interpret literary accounts of what I call erotic care of the soul. Erotic care of the soul is a form of regenerative, body-focused healing in the tradition of the ministry of Jesus. It constitutes physical expressions of love of the flesh

---

1 Gloria Naylor's depiction of Mattie bathing Ceil, Toni Morrison's inclusion of Baby Suggs washing Sethe, and Alice Walker's bathing of Shug Avery are just a few instances of Black women bathing one another in the literary tradition of Black women. For more, see Gloria Naylor, *The Women of Brewster Place* (New York: Penguin, 1982); Toni Morrison, *Beloved* (New York: Vintage, 1987); and Alice Walker, *The Color Purple: A Novel* (New York: Harcourt Brace Jovanovich, 1982).

2 Cannon, *Black Womanist Ethics*, 7.

that, when executed by and upon Black women, minister to what womanist ethicist Emilie Townes calls the *isness*[3] of Black female being. Through acts of care, it affirms the worth and divinity of Black female corporeality. So too, I argue that scenes of Black women bathing each other posit erotic care as an effective moral formula for reconciling disintegrated aspects of Black personhood.

This chapter also aims to contribute to womanist knowledge of the erotic within and beyond sex. While womanist scholars freely acknowledge that the erotic is more than sexual sensation but a life force located in the union of spirit and flesh that manifests love, rarely, if ever, do they attend to the vitality of the erotic outside of a sexual context.[4] By investigating literary accounts of Black women bathing in both sexual and nonsexual contexts, this chapter recovers Black women's attitudes regarding the erotic charge present in varying dynamics of touch and its efficacy in generating what I call corporeal conscientization. My contribution to womanist ethics' lexicon on the erotic, *corporeal conscientization* is a term I have coined to describe the impact of the erotic on stigmatized bodies and its effect on Black female moral agency. A joyful product of erotic care/the ministry of touch, I argue, corporeal conscientization accomplishes an epistemological shift that imbues Black female flesh with new meaning and calls the body, will, and spirit estranged by the traumas of dehumanization back into relationship.

Black historian of religion Charles H. Long contends, "As stepchildren of Western culture . . . the experiences of the oppressed were rooted in the absurd meaning of their bodies, and it was for these bodies that they were regarded not only as valuable works, but also as the locus of the ideologies that justified their enslavement."[5] Demonized by bodily difference, Black rational capacity, morality, and virtue—the very constitution of Black being—have been maligned on account of the flesh that incarnates them.

---

3 Emilie Townes, *In a Blaze of Glory: Womanist Spirituality as Social Witness* (Nashville: Abingdon, 1995), 11. Townes describes *isness* as the intersection of the spiritual and physical components of their being, which results in a deeply embodied spirituality that honors the wholeness and continuity of the human experience and seeks transformation in the concrete realities of Black people. A spirituality that involves both body and soul, isness unifies the sacrality of what is reserved for the divine with the everyday experiences of humanity.

4 Baker-Fletcher, "The Erotic in Contemporary Black Women's Writings"; Day, *Resistance to Neoliberalism*, 77.

5 Long, *Significations*, 211.

These bodies serve as both the source of white animus and the terrain upon which it was meted out. More than the subject of disparaging ideologies in the atmosphere, the flesh of Black people has been whittled, seared, pummeled, and violently dispossessed in the process of degradation from human being to nonbeing. Baring what literary critic Hortense Spillers calls the hieroglyphics of the flesh, the wounds that the material bodies of Black people hold are a testament to their grievously violent transformation from human beings to chattel. Moreover, these wounds allude to the psychic scars whose healing goes beyond declarations of wholeness and the manipulation of ideologies. The physical trauma visited upon Black people festers as a communal wound of bodily shame and alienation. This wound represents a sickness that is unto death, signaling a need for a vehicle of reincarnation, so that life may be born afresh.

Through scenes of the erotic care of bathing, Black female novelists not only rewrite Black women's bodies as sacred but also present the mysterious power of the erotic, for which Black women have been maligned, as the divine capacity that resides within them to redeem flesh and invigorate the will. For example, Black female writer Gloria Naylor's novel *Women of Brewster Place* offers a riveting depiction of the capacity of erotic care to resuscitate wills exhausted by the hopelessness of Black women's existential crises. Naylor writes,

Mattie stood in the doorway, and an involuntary shudder went through her when she saw Ciel's eyes. Dear God, she's dying, and right in front of our faces. . . . No! no! no! Like a Brahman cow, desperate to protect her young, she surged into the room. . . .

She sat on the edge of the bed and enfolded the tissue thin body in her huge ebony arms. And she rocked.

Ciel's body was so hot it burned Mattie when she first touched her, but she held on and rocked. Back and forth back and forth—she held Ciel so tightly, she could feel her young breast flatten against the buttons of her dress. . . . She rocked.

And somewhere from the bowels of Ciel's being came a moan so high it couldn't be heard by anyone, but the yard dog began an unholy howling. And Mattie rocked; and agonizingly slow it broke its way through the parched lips . . . Ciel moaned. Mattie rocked. She rocked her into her childhood and let her see her murdered dreams, she rocked her back, back into the womb to the nadir of the hurt. And she rocked and pulled until the splinter of pain gave way, but its roots were deep, gigantic and ragged and it left a huge hole which had already starting to pus over, but Mattie was satisfied. It would heal.

> Mattie then drew a tub of hot water and undressed Ciel. . . . And she
> slowly bathed her. She washed her hair and the back of her neck. . . . She
> let the soap between the girl's breasts . . . soaped her pubic hair, and gen-
> tly washed the creases of her vagina—slowly, reverently, as if handling a
> newborn baby.[6]

Mattie, a displaced Black woman who loses her home after her son jumps bail, resurrects Ciel's will for real living through intimate bodily care that reaches beyond the physical to touch her wounded spirit. Ciel, having just lost her daughter, "the only thing she has loved without pain," in a freak accident, is so consumed by grief she is despondent.[7] Her state can serve as a metaphor for many Black women whose experiences of trauma, induced by poverty, racism, and the constant suppression of their own needs for the needs of others, cause dissociation—a disconnection or rupture between the mind, body, and spirit. Emotionally vacant and absent of will, Ciel sits, not as a person, but as a mound of flesh with no will to fight. While the precipitating event for Ciel's breakdown is the death of her daughter, the circumstances that surround the baby's death—the dilapidated nature of the tenement apartment to which her family was confined, her boyfriend's unemployment, the emotional abuse she suffered within the toxic relationship, and the very fight between them that distracted Ciel from more diligently watching her daughter—can all be directly linked to the absurd and consuming conditions of oppression provoked by racism, sexism, and classism. Ciel's hopeless despondence, while extreme, is not an uncommon posture. In fact, many Black women take on variations of disintegration, numbing themselves psychically and emotionally and disconnecting themselves from their bodies as they attempt to survive the devastating suffering and anguish of feeling responsible for the circumstances of their lives, yet utterly powerless to change them.[8]

The disintegrative effects of dissociation are a product of the denigration and dispossession of Black women and men from the status of human being to commodified, degenerate, impotent other, produced by their pornographic encounter with the Western world. Pornographic in the sense, as

---

6 Naylor, *The Women of Brewster Place*, 104.

7 Naylor, *The Women of Brewster Place*, 93.

8 For more, see Lorde, "Uses of the Erotic"; Walker-Barnes, *Too Heavy a Yoke*; and Phillis Sheppard, *Self, Culture, and Others in Womanist Practical Theology* (New York: Palgrave Macmillan, 2011). Each chronicles Black women's dissociation as numbing, a stifling of emotions, and the formal psychological malady respectively.

Black feminist poet Audre Lorde writes, that it renders them bodies without feelings, Black Africans' encounter with Western man separated Black bodies from the fullness of their sentience, disintegrating Black subjecthood, such that the sensory capacity of enslaved bodies was present, but their emotional, psychological, and psychic subjectivity was silenced.[9]

Disintegration shows up in Black women's strategies of survival as well. In his essay "The Spirit Is Willing, and the Flesh Is Too," practical theologian Lee Butler discusses the tactic of "separating what we perceive to be ourselves from our bodies in the midst of struggle" deployed by many in the Black community.[10] Explaining the logic of disintegration, he writes, "If we simply separate ourselves from the body, then the condition of the body is of no consequence."[11] The propensity for body/soul bifurcation is not only a legacy of Christianity's suspicion of the body but is, as Butler explains, a troubling response to violations of the human soul that cause us to frequently separate ourselves from our bodies, cognitively and emotionally, in order to escape the horrors of victimization.[12]

To escape the absurd meanings of the body, Butler contends that Black people overly spiritualize their lives and sacrifice their sexualities, resulting in a division that erodes the unity of Black being and their ability to be relational beings.[13] While his primary focus is the sexual nature of detachment, Ciel's circumstances depict detachment and its death-dealing implications as a response to emotional anguish, too often visited upon Black women. Ciel vacates her body, in an attempt to silence not her sexuality but the pain and grief that reside *in* her body and *on* account of her body. Her dissociation is an attempt to seek respite from the sensory ache of all of life's losses—her innocence, her ability to dream, her partner, her beloved daughter, her power to make anything different. This tactic, however, does not contribute to her survival, but her impending demise. As Mattie exclaims, "She is dying right before our eyes!"[14] Ciel's dissociation is emblematic of the many Black people who, in response to their dehumanization, lapse into a liminal space of constrained sentient existence, suppressing the human impulse to feel and desire, in effect dehumanizing

---

9 Lorde, "Uses of the Erotic," 88.
10 Butler, "The Spirit Is Willing but the Flesh Is Weak," 114.
11 Butler, "The Spirit Is Willing but the Flesh Is Weak," 114.
12 Butler, "The Spirit Is Willing but the Flesh Is Weak," 114.
13 Butler, "The Spirit Is Willing but the Flesh Is Weak," 114.
14 Naylor, *The Women of Brewster Place*, 104.

themselves because the anguish of their existence is too much to bear.[15] Her inability to register feeling, I argue, is Naylor's well-crafted illustration of the rupture of the mind-body connection typical of people who feel powerless. Lifeless, existing void of affect, Ciel finds her will extinguished under the crushing weight of the burden of Black womanhood. Ciel's erotic baptism, however, signals the possibility of redemption—a redemption whose power relies upon the body.

Through erotic care of the soul, Mattie snatches Ciel from the jaws of hopelessness. Her manner of bringing Ceil back to life demands Mattie's bodily participation, undressing, bathing, washing, handling Ciel's body as sacred. "Reverently," Naylor writes, Mattie attends to even the parts of Ciel's body that have been culturally and religiously coded as evil, blurring the lines of the sacred and the sexual. As a result, Ciel is healed. Her healing is signaled not in her standing triumphantly, but through tears that spilled over her body, baptizing them again in the reconciliation of her body and her spirit. In his explanation of haptology, the theology of touch, Mark Wallace argues, "The well-being for someone else's flesh is the grounds for salvation and forgiveness in God's new order of being."[16] Wallace maintains only through physical acts of receiving and giving love can defiled flesh be restored. Based in part on Toni Morrison's account of erotic care in her novel *Beloved*, "a kind of African derived, body-loving, nature-based religion" used by former slaves to heal themselves, Wallace's haptology posits to the restorative power of the erotic—the manifestation of love, sexual and nonsexual, in and through the flesh and its capacity to heal those disfigured physically and psychologically from the wounds of violence motivated by racial difference.[17] Wallace maintains that defiled flesh can be restored through physical acts of receiving and giving love. Erotic encounters, he argues, hold "the potential to heal our culture of its penchant for abuse of one another's flesh and to teach us to love our own and others' innermost desires for pleasure, intimacy, friendship and love."[18]

Wallace's haptology fits squarely with womanist theologian M. Shawn Copeland's theology of eros as embodied spirituality. Copeland emphasizes

---

15 Butler, "The Spirit Is Willing but the Flesh Is Weak," 114.
16 Wallace, "Early Christian Contempt for the Flesh," 41.
17 Wallace, "Early Christian Contempt for the Flesh," 46.
18 Wallace, "Early Christian Contempt for the Flesh," 34.

the centrality of Jesus's body in his ministry on earth, writing, "He gave his body, his very self, to and for others."[19] Jesus's eros for humanity governs much of his healing ministry on earth, Copeland argues, such that Jesus operates as a divine union of spirit and flesh, seeking after humanity for hospitable and sacrificial action facilitated by bodily love and intimacy.[20] Echoing the sentiments of Audre Lorde, in her seminal essay "Uses of the Erotic," Copeland describes eros as a creative life force that motivates and incites Jesus's sacrificial action, through embodied hospitality, welcoming the marginalized into physical and emotional intimacy.[21] In other words, with his body, Jesus communicates his desire for communion with those who have been socially alienated, drawing them back into community and relationship, loving their being through care for their bodies, and asserting God's fundamental desire for unity with God's people.

Wallace explains that throughout his ministry, Jesus enacted the erotic as hospitality, offering his body as a gift as he invited the dispossessed and disconnected into physical intimacy with him. His bodily offering made the real (sensually discernable) presence of God available to those to whom he ministered.[22] Copeland specifies that in many instances it was the oppressed, those excluded from society as a result of social status and illness, with whom Jesus shared physical intimacy. As such, Jesus's eros preempts the social order's alienation of the oppressed, as God's indiscriminate love of the world enacted through his erotic hospitality upends the hierarchical schemas that stigmatize and marginalize bodies marked by economic, religious, and social factors. Copeland offers,

> At the center of Jesus' praxis were the bodies of common people. Peasants, economic and political refugees, the poor and the destitute. They were the subjects of his compassionate care: children, women, and men who were materially impoverished, as well as those who were socially and religiously marginalized, or were physically disabled. . . . Jesus did not shun or despise these women and men; he put his body where they were. He handled, touched and embraced their marked bodies. Jesus befriended them.[23]

---

19 Copeland, *Enfleshing Freedom*, 65.
20 Copeland, *Enfleshing Freedom*, 65.
21 Copeland, *Enfleshing Freedom*, 64–65.
22 Wallace, "Early Christian Contempt for the Flesh," 48–49.
23 Copeland, *Enfleshing Freedom*, 60.

Copeland describes the interactions Jesus has with the bodies of others as "intimate encounters."[24] Such intimacy enacts the exchange Wallace proffers for the restoration of defiled flesh, making it an emollient of the psychic wounds of social degradation and stigma. Through these intimate encounters, Jesus enacts erotic care of the soul, imparting relational and psychic healing and power to those with whom he shares physical intimacy. I argue Jesus's haptic engagement of marginalized flesh recalibrates the identities of those systematically alienated by and from society, restoring their sense of worth, belonging, and purpose. His touch challenges empire's pornographic defiling and disorienting treatment of oppressed bodies, redeeming them from stigma, valorizing them as God's beloved, and reintegrating them into community.

Throughout his ministry, Jesus erotically cared for the souls of the outcast—healing, redeeming, regenerating, and reintegrating them for the pleasure of reuniting them to community and restoring them to wholeness. In this way, I contend, Jesus's ministry on earth is a form of erotic defiance, in that he demonstrates great love/concern for and pleasure in not only the souls of the oppressed, marginalized, and stigmatized but also their bodies—their material being—and invites those who identify with him to do the same in resistance to the socio-religious hierarchies operative in his time.

THE ROLE OF EMBODIMENT IN IDENTITY

Dispossession of the body colors all aspects of Black consciousness and identity. This is a function of the body's role in identity construction. Philosopher Merleau-Ponty argues that the disclosure of the world is experienced though the body. For him, human experience is the product of the relationship between the subject and the world (that which appears before him or her in a given setting). This relationship is impossible without the body—the subject of experience and perception. "The world is not what I think, but what I live through," Merleau-Ponty writes.[25] He posits that the world as the contextual backdrop or setting of existence establishes a horizon, or scope, of meaning for all things. Accordingly, disclosure of the world

---

24 Marcella Althaus-Reid, *Indecent Theology: Theological Perversions in Sex, Gender and Politics* (London: Routledge, 2000), 113.

25 Merleau-Ponty, *Phenomenology of Perception*, 407.

through the body's experience of material phenomena through the senses grounds consciousness and identity. He explains,

> Insofar as, when I reflect on the essence of subjectivity, I find it bound up with that of the body and that of the world, this is because my existence as subjectivity is merely one with my existence as a body and with the existence of the world, and because the subject I am, when taken concretely, is inseparable from this body and this world.[26]

Underscoring the interdependent relationship between the body and the world as the ground of subjectivity, Merleau-Ponty avers that consciousness transcends the limits of the rational and is understood as an embodied undertaking. As such, he argues, subjectivity is dependent on embodiment, and identity becomes a product of the experiencing body-subject in the world.

While Merleau-Ponty's insistence on the body as self in the world positions the body as the means by which the world is apprehended by a subject, it does not account for how the specificity of said bodies impacts experience and the ways these experiences construct a sense of identity. As Merleau-Ponty and later phenomenologists Howard Harrod and Robert Sokolowski point out, as agents apprehend the world, they do so with and through their bodies. The reaction to these bodies, based on phenotypical markers like race and sex, orients the reception of bodyselves—the opportunities and exposure given to them, the way they are handled, and the limits imposed upon them. Womanist ethicist Katie Cannon's words offer specifics on the particularities of the Black body's situatedness in the world and its impact on Black existence:

> Black existence is deliberately and openly controlled . . . "how we travel and where, what work we do, what income we receive, where we eat, where we sleep, with whom we talk, we recreate, where we study, what we write, what we publish . . ." The vast majority of blacks suffer every conceivable form of denigration. Their lives are named, defined and circumscribed by whites.[27]

Cannon brings to the fore the drastically all-encompassing effect of white supremacy on the subjectivity of Black people. She articulates the devastating reach and control of the culture of racism on the lives of Black people as more than just an occasional nuisance, but a principal element of the experience

---

26 Merleau-Ponty, *Phenomenology of Perception*, 408–9.

27 Katie Cannon, *Katie's Canon: Womanism and the Soul of the Black Community* (New York: Bloomsbury, 1998), 59.

of the world for Black people that limits and confines every aspect of their social being.

If we apply phenomenological logic to the circumstances of Black people, it can be argued that the confinement of one's being and the ideologies that facilitate such treatment must have tremendous implications on the construction of Black identity. However, the racial and gendered aspects of what Harrod and Sokolowski call embodied sociality—the social dimension of the subject informed by one's embodiment, which contributes to the ways human agents construct and codify value intersubjectively (in community and in agreement with other selves in the social world)—go unnamed in their work.[28]

Harrod and Sokolowski contend that it is the mutual intention (attention to and understanding) of objects in the world (our bodies included) that grounds our sociality. As objects in the world, raced and gendered bodies are assigned value intersubjectively. However, M. Shawn Copeland argues, "The body mediates our engagement with others, with the world and with the Other."[29] This mediation is facilitated by the symbolic meanings of bodies. She writes, "The social body's assignment of meaning and significance to race and/or gender and/or sexuality to physical bodies influences, perhaps even determines, the trajectories of concrete lives."[30] In other words, our interpersonal engagements are calibrated by our cultural perceptions of different types of bodies. Moreover, the predetermined perceptions of those bodies have institutional and structural ramifications, dictating how particular bodies will be treated, educated, and cared for, as well as the opportunities that will be provided for them.

EROTIC CARE AS A REORIENTATION OF IDENTITY

For many, including some of the most celebrated and influential theorists of Black culture, the experience of racism is the foundational phenomenon of theories of Black psychology and identity. However, in her book *Toward a Womanist Ethic of Incarnation: Black Bodies, the Black Church, and the Council of Chalcedon*, womanist ethicist Eboni Marshall Turman characterizes

---

28 For more on sociality, see Robert Sokolowski, *Introduction to Phenomenology* (Cambridge: Cambridge University Press, 2000); and Harrod, *Human Center*.

29 Copeland, *Enfleshing Freedom*, 7.

30 Copeland, *Enfleshing Freedom*, 8.

the tradition of constructing Black identity as a reaction to racial oppression as detrimental. She specifically lifts W. E. B. Du Bois's dialectical theories of double consciousness and the veil.[31] Critiquing Du Bois's formulation of Black subjectivity as derivative of white notions of Blackness, Marshall Turman contends, "The thrust of Du Bois's argumentation concerning *the souls of black folk* is paradoxically contingent on the *kata sarka* gaze of a white girl."[32] Privileging an *en sarki dei* approach, Marshall Turman argues that the incarnation suggests that personhood is established by the primary activity of God in the flesh. Accordingly, she contends that isness is divinely established. Rather than constructed by what happens to a subject, "it is a given, demanded by what happens *en sarki*."[33] On the contrary, Marshall Turman argues, "Du Bois's assertion concerning *dark bodies* 'born with a veil and gifted with second sight'" follows a *kata sarka* orientation of identity, which "problematically confines the breadth and depth of black flesh to its contentious relationality with the white gaze."[34] Such formulations, Marshall Turman argues, severely delimit Black identity, rendering it a mere reaction to the perspectives of an adversarial other and the actions inflicted upon Black bodies. Through her *en sarki dei* approach to Black identity, Marshall Turman privileges the presence and activity of God in the flesh of Black people, particularly Black women, beyond the historical atrocities they have endured, as a means of communicating the sacrality, virtue, beauty, and fullness of their being.

While Marshall Turman critiques constructions of identity that too heavily rely on what has happened to the body from a sociohistorical lens, the works

---

31 Du Bois's theory of double consciousness is introduced in his seminal text *The Souls of Black Folk*. It articulates the existential conundrum of perceiving oneself through the eyes of whiteness. Du Bois argues, "The history of the American Negro is the history of this strife—this longing to attain self-conscious manhood, to merge his double self into a better and truer self." Du Bois, *Souls of Black Folk*, 3.

32 Eboni Marshall Turman, *Toward a Womanist Ethic of Incarnation: Black Bodies, the Black Church, and the Council of Chalcedon* (New York: Palgrave Macmillan, 2013), 86. *Kata sarka* or "according to the flesh," based on what happens to Jesus's flesh in history, and *en sarki dei*, in which the nature and identity of Jesus is established based on God's activity in the flesh of Jesus, are Chalcedonian categories proposed by the Alexandrian Church at the Council of Chalcedon and the Council of Nicea respectively, to describe the nature and identity of Jesus. Marshall Turman argues these categories are paradigmatic of approaches to Black identity.

33 Marshall Turman, *Toward a Womanist Ethic of Incarnation*, 18.

34 Marshall Turman, *Toward a Womanist Ethic of Incarnation*, 3.

of Sheppard and Crumpton prove a necessary intervention because they highlight the importance of the specificity of bodies in the phenomenological concept of embodied sociality. Black women's experiences of their bodies in the world lead to their apprehension of the world as a toxic environment and the perception of their bodies as less esteemed than other bodies in society. This intersubjectively generated value, in turn, funds Black women's identity construction. For example, in the recently replicated famous Black and white doll experiment, Black children pronounce the pejorative meanings of Black skin and its correspondence with bad or immoral character.[35]

What we do with our bodies ratifies or challenges the construction of the hegemonic imagination,[36] particularly the effects of bodily stigma on the people it degrades. Therefore, it is imperative that Black women have opportunities to experience themselves as something other than inferior, problematic, or immoral, for they contribute to a healthier self-concept. These opportunities, I maintain, require the intentional curating of life-giving sociality, with special emphasis on modes of erotic relationality that offer new value meanings to Black women's corporeality. Through these acts, I argue, the significance of Blackness and the impact of racial identity on the psyches of Black Americans in both a social and spiritual context are recalibrated. Contesting the fallacies of the collective cultural imagination that haunt our self-concept, Black women's practices of erotic care subvert empire's pornographic power through loving encounter with each other's bodies. These acts of care, I argue, valorize and authorize Black flesh through the witness of Black women's bodies as the embodiment of God's loving activity in the here and now.

Through participation in erotic care, the significance of Black women's flesh as both recipient and healer undergoes transformation, whereby the power of the spirit flows from one body to another, serving as a reminder of the activity of God within. As such, the sanctity of their bodies is reaffirmed.

---

35 Diane Byrd et al., "A Modern Doll Study: Self Concept," *Race, Gender & Class* 24, nos. 1–2 (2017): 186–202.

36 Townes, *Womanist Ethics*, 7. Townes contends that the fantastic hegemonic imagination, the psychological engine that drives the ideas we have about particular groups, and therefore injustice, transforms real people into caricatures. These caricatures provide the psychological distance between reality and fantasy necessary for the evil of "isms" to persist. Encouraging the masses to maintain the physical distance necessary to keep society ignorant of real life and faithful to the images conjured by the fantastic hegemonic imagination, these caricatures/stereotypes dictate the ways we relate to one another.

Such power seems an impossibility, yet I argue the same oppressed Black body that provides for the material manifestation of white supremacy can through strategies of counter creative signification materially contest the myth of white supremacy, as well as play a key role in identity construction through erotic care.

From a theological perspective, the experience and deployment of the erotic make evident the connection between body and spirit, which connect us with the presence of God's spirit within—our ability to love and to feel passionately, our will and our desire. The erotic's regenerative effect signals a relationship between it and the Holy Spirit. Ascribed the power of regeneration in the Bible, the Holy Spirit is the presence of the power of the Lord that enables Jesus to heal (Luke 5:17b). However, even when the presence of God goes unnamed, loving encounters of the flesh impart meaning, declaring the value of the bodies being cared for as beloved and disclosing these bodies as principal resources in the apprehension of knowledge and the shaping of identity.

If loving touch loves flesh back to life, the spirit of God redeems it back to wholeness. Together they constitute the erotic's work of redeeming, reorienting, and connecting alienated beings with the community and the spirit of God and manifesting the materiality of love. I liken this work to an exorcism of sorts, calling the demons of self-hatred out of the Black psyche and commandeering the authority of white ideology. The witness of Black women offering erotic care to other Black women discloses the erotic's capacity to resuscitate annihilated personhood through affirmation, regeneration, and reintegration. It affirms the body as good, worthy of care, a resource for knowledge, and the site of pleasure through sensory experience. Through this, I argue the erotic annuls the psychic pain of bodily shame instilled by racial oppression by offering Black flesh occasions to be received and declared as both valued members of the Black community and the community of God. These experiences, I contend, are vital to the livelihood and psyches of Black people. Through erotic care Black women employ one of the only resources they have—their bodies, laying hands on each other to survive, to be revived, and to be connected to God and their community as they continue in their ongoing fight to remember their identity, their gifts, and their sacred worth.

Returning to Marshall Turman's paradigm of Black identity construction, erotic care of the soul can be understood as a ritual context for conscientization that reorients Black subjectivities from a *kata sarka* approach to identity to an *en sarki dei* approach. In other words, it accomplishes an epistemological shift that establishes identity based upon what God has done in the bodies of Black women as opposed to what has happened to their bodies.[37] Privileging the activity of God in the flesh of Black women, erotic care is the embodiment of womanist ethicist Stacey Floyd-Thomas's concept of traditional communalism.[38] Born out of Black women's sense of solidarity with and responsibility for each other, traditional communalism as defined by Floyd-Thomas is the transferal of wisdom, intended to emancipate Black women from warped theological anthropologies, promulgated by Western notions of humanness. The wisdom offered is a byproduct of Black women's navigation of tripartite oppression. I contend that in the case of erotic care, Black women subvert empire's pornographic power through transformative experiences of loving encounter with each other's bodies.

An example of erotic care's capacity to heal and enliven the will is found in the novel *Beloved*, in which Toni Morrison articulates the importance of touch in the African American folk context as the materiality of love.[39] Woven throughout the narrative of Sethe, a self-emancipated mother who survived slavery, Morrison depicts the community's use of their hands to communicate intimacy, care, and praise. Literary critic Anissa Janine Wardi writes, "It is the actions of the hands that materialize love."[40] While Wardi is correct, I argue that the hands are not the only actors in the communication of love, but the body as a whole. In acts of healing veneration, Baby Suggs, Sethe's mother-in-law, used her body in some of the most erotic and intimate ways to care for Sethe:

> Sethe remembered the touch of those fingers that she knew better than her own. They bathed her in sections, wrapped her womb, combed her hair, oiled her nipples, stitched her clothes, cleaned her feet, greased her back and dropped just about anything they were doing to massage Sethe's nape when, especially in the

---

37 Marshall Turman, *Toward a Womanist Ethic of Incarnation*, 48.

38 Traditional communalism is solidarity with and preference for Black women's culture, and the wisdom and knowledge for survival and liberation that accompany it. For more, see Stacey Floyd-Thomas, *Deeper Shades of Purple: Womanism in Religion and Society* (New York: New York University Press, 2006), 78.

39 Anissa Janine Wardi, "A Laying On of Hands: Toni Morrison and the Materiality of Love," *MELUS* 30.3 (2005): 201–18.

40 Wardi, "A Laying On of Hands," 201.

early days her spirits fell down under the weight of the things she remembered and those she did not.[41]

These material signs of love and healing sear with intimacy, queering traditional conceptions of eros as Baby Suggs attends to the most private parts of Sethe's body—her genitals, her head, her feet, the nape of her neck—acknowledging the sacrality of the various parts of her body and affirming Sethe's sense of worth. These acts, which fortify the hallowed kinship she and Baby Suggs share with each other, tend to the sexually intimate parts of Sethe, but they do not intend to arouse sexual pleasure. I contend that the sexual nature of the abuse and diminishment Sethe endured make the locus of Baby Suggs's care appropriate. Imparting a kind of motherly love, Suggs communicates to Sethe the value of every part of her body and her being as something worthy of being cherished and preserved.

Baby Suggs's healing touch affirms a sacred connection between her body and Sethe's, fostering a sense of solidarity and psychic bonds. Furthermore, the act valorizes Baby Sugg's body as an agent of love and redemptive power and Sethe's body as beloved. In these practices of erotic care, Sethe finds the peace and security necessary to live and hope again. Baby Suggs's rituals of healing function as Sethe's way back from nobodyness to being human again. Baby Suggs's humanity is also reaffirmed.

Meeting one another at the locus of crisis—their bodies—these rituals of erotic care valorize and authorize Black female flesh through the activity and testimony of their own bodies, and defy the narratives of Black womanhood perpetuated by racist patriarchy. Through these experiences and the sacramentality of Black women who operate as caregivers, erotic care of the soul accomplishes a dramatic epistemological shift in how recipients of care understand their bodies and their identities. Triggering the construction of a radical subjectivity undergirded by a belief in God's activity in the bodies and encounters of Black women, I maintain that erotic care counters the claims of the *kata sarka* scandal of Black womanhood.

If the pornographic handling of white institutions and flesh animated by white supremacy denigrates Black people, then erotic care of the soul

---

41 Morrison, *Beloved*, 98.

resuscitates them through positive and pleasurable experiences of their body-selves as beloved by and connected to the community/God. Acting as ambassadors of God's redeeming love, Black women make the divine present in the temporal realm. The sacramental nature of Black women's bodies is a central feature in womanist religious scholarship.[42] For example, Eboni Marshall Turman attests that Black women's bodies are the incarnate image of God in the world, sharing in the same ethical substance of Christ.[43] For Marshall Turman, Black women's sameness with Christ exists in their activity, specifically their postures of renunciation, inclusion, and responsibility. While Marshall Turman takes her cue from womanist ethicist Marcia Riggs, who emphasizes renunciation as an exercise of renouncing privilege, if we take a more expansive approach, renunciation can be applied to any behavior or belief that opposes God's intention for human relationality.[44] This certainly includes the hoarding of privilege but can also include the refusal of ideologies that desecrate the image of God in the oppressed.

As such, Black women's erotic care is an exercise in bodily inclusion and renunciation. It defies their demonization through the very object of their vilification—their supposedly evil, contaminated, and contagious bodies. As they lay hands on each other, the power of the spirit flows from one body to another, emblematic of their similitude with Jesus's ontological status as the union of the flesh and the divine. Like Jesus, in collaboration with the Spirit, Black women subvert empire's pornographic power as agents of the eros of God, valorizing and authorizing Black flesh as good ground, worthy of being used and cared for by God. As a result, the significance of their flesh, as both healer and recipient, is transformed. Bathing their sisters, Black women minister to despised flesh in the spirit of Jesus, reflexively restoring dignity and revealing the divine rather than the detrimental nature of their contagion. Such renunciation is made possible by bodily hospitality that, like Jesus, renounces faulty constructions that declare them unworthy and invalid through embodied hospitality that gives way to the experience of being beloved.

While the power of the Spirit residing in Black women provides the divine power of erotic care, the experience and bodily pleasure of being

---

42 To understand one's body as sacramental is to believe that one's body is a material sign or symbol of God's presence. However, more than merely symbolic, Black women's bodies are perceived as vessels of God's presence and activity.

43 Marshall Turman, *Toward a Womanist Ethic of Incarnation*, 161.

44 Marshall Turman, *Toward a Womanist Ethic of Incarnation*, 161.

beloved, communicated through bodily hospitality, provides the portal. Through erotic touch, flesh loves flesh back to life and restores the disintegrated back to wholeness. This collaboration of Spirit and flesh constitutes the erotic's work of reconciliation, reconnecting alienated beings to God, each other, and themselves through acts that manifest love materially.[45] Upholding the ethical postures of renunciation and inclusion of Jesus, erotic care provides for those who have been victims of bodily deprecation essential opportunities to experience their bodies beyond moral dilemma. Such experiences are transformative, not only to Black female identity, but to their moral agency as well.

To understand the erotic's impact on moral agency, an understanding of moral agency beyond the context of normative Western ethical thought, that is, Aristotelian, Augustinian, and Kantian moral philosophies is necessary. Moral agency—the capacity of an individual to make judgments and choices that best suit his or her good, or the good of the community—has traditionally been approached as a disembodied phenomenon.[46] Theorized as a function of the mind, the rational aspects of moral agency have maintained centrality, while the body has been perceived as an obstacle to overcome. Consequently, the body's contribution to moral agency, prior to action, is absent in many Western moral philosophies. Womanist practical theologians Phillis Sheppard and Stephanie Crumpton advance the ideas of phenomenologists like Maurice Merleau-Ponty, Howard Harrod, and Robert Sokolowski who challenge formulations of moral agency that neglect the body by emphasizing its function in experience as agents apprehend the world.[47] While Merleau-Ponty, Harrod, and Sokolowski amplify the body's contributions to the constitution of consciousness/subjectivity and the construction of meaning, Sheppard and Crumpton underscore the importance of the specificity of bodies in the phenomenological concept of embodied sociality.[48] Womanist methodological approaches, in conjunction with a phenomenological approach, inspire the reading of Black women's bodies as texts, shifting my attention to practices,

---

45 Wardi, "A Laying On of Hands."

46 For more, see Linda Holler, *Erotic Morality: The Role of Touch in Moral Agency* (New Brunswick, NJ: Rutgers University Press, 2002), 8–10; and Robert Sokolowski, *Moral Action: A Phenomenological Study* (Bloomington: Indiana University Press, 1985), 48–54.

47 Sokolowski, *Introduction to Phenomenology*, 11–16.

48 For more, see Sheppard, *Self, Culture, and Others*, 57; and Stephanie Crumpton, *A Womanist Pastoral Theology against Intimate and Cultural Violence* (New York: Palgrave Macmillan, 2014), 84–91.

or the ethics of the body as a kind of discourse. These methodologies, I argue, disclose how the signifying language of ethics operative in cultural productions like religious rituals; Black female musicians' creative expression and navigation of racial, gender, and sexual politics; and political engagement serve as both spiritual and secular testimony, revealing their didactic functions in the Black communities.

Embodied sociality, the social dimension of the subject informed by one's embodiment, contributes to the ways human agents construct and codify value intersubjectively (in community and in agreement with other selves in the social world).[49] However, Sheppard points out that Black women's experiences of their bodies in the world lead to their apprehension of the world as a toxic environment and the perception of their bodies as less esteemed than other bodies in society.[50] This intersubjectively generated value, in turn, calibrates Black women's identity construction. Consequently, opportunities for Black women to experience themselves as something other than inferior, problematic, or immoral immediately contribute to a healthier self-concept. As Black women's literature demonstrates, such opportunities offer new value meanings to Black women's bodies as beloved, sacred subjects and agents of divine love and healing.

To be called beloved, womanist ethicist Emilie Townes argues, is a call to self-love and respect for radical isness in the context of African American life.[51] Erotic care communicates belovedness, allowing Black women to experience their bodies beyond moral dilemma, that is, stigmatization and oppression; erotic care, sexual and nonsexual, declares what had been categorized as corrupt and obscene to be worthy of love and ratified as valid. As Wallace's and Copeland's analyses of Jesus's hospitality attest, erotic care is potent with transformative power both through the power of the Spirit that resides in the body and the body-affirming experiences of inclusion and pleasure they provide. The embodied hospitality of erotic care calls subjects into belovedness—that is, the experience of being desired, reached for, and drawn close in all their isness.[52] This invitation preempts the alienation, stigmatization, and degradation imposed by a society and culture that intends Black women harm. Relevant to this chapter is the way belovedness, communicated through inclusion, is experienced in the body. The delight of physical participation with the bodies of others, the touch of belonging and inclusion, and

---

49 Harrod, *Human Center*; Sokolowski, *Introduction to Phenomenology*.
50 Sheppard, *Self, Culture, and Others*, 57.
51 Townes, *In a Blaze of Glory*, 48.
52 Townes, *In a Blaze of Glory*, 11.

the joy of offering it underscore the body's role as the site of pleasure as well as a resource for new knowledge that one discovers through the senses. This sense data, received through the experience of being undressed, bathed, and cherished, as sacred gifts, imparts erotic pleasure that reaches beyond the flesh and calls Black women into seeing themselves as bodies worthy of love from others and therefore themselves. Such revelation disrupts traditional values imposed upon them by refuting the authority of fabricated ideologies that render Black women a problem.[53] Reminiscent of Paulo Freire's theory of conscientization, erotic care engenders a corporeal awareness or consciousness of the body as loved, desired, and valid, and of its role as an arbiter of this sensory knowledge.

Equally important are the ways these erotic acts call participants into, as Townes explains, "respect for radical isness."[54] Townes's concept of isness holds together the disparate parts of Black female being, often dissociated by the traumas of Black women's pornographic encounters with the caustic environs of Western civilization. Townes contends that erotic care is communicated through loving physical touch, so pleasurable, it calls Black women to self-love and radical isness. She asserts, "To love one's body," a body that has been dubbed accursed, "is radical spirituality within structured dominion and control."[55] To love said body and maintain the integrity of its connection to the mind and soul is a posture of resistance made possible through corporeal conscientization of eros.

Preacher Monya Stubbs exemplifies the cohering and conscientizing activity of eros in her own life as she narrates how her mother's erotic care became

---

53 Institutional power generates the kind of knowledge it needs to be sustained. French philosopher Michel Foucault calls this "the will to knowledge." To produce this knowledge, power enlists various kinds of intelligence like science and theology to disseminate the ideas it seeks to construct. The Age of Enlightenment was characterized by the pursuit of knowledge and the freedom to do so unencumbered by religious limitations. During this time, science became increasingly revered, while religion lost its authoritative advantage. Christian philosophers, looking for a way to maintain Christianity's influence in an increasingly skeptical world, collaborated with the ideologies and sciences of the day in the denigration of Black bodies. Christianity theologically legitimated the subordination of Black people through the construction of a morality grounded in the perceived inferiority of their rational capacity and their physical appearances. Accordingly, bodies which approximated to the Greco-Roman aesthetic and subjects who submitted to Western notions of appropriateness and rationality were deemed valid human subjects. For more, see Foucault, *History of Sexuality*, 3:101. For more on the discursive denigration of Black people, see West, "Genealogy of Modern Racism"; and Douglas, *What's Faith Got to Do With It?*, 113–27.
54 Townes, *In a Blaze of Glory*, 48.
55 Townes, *In a Blaze of Glory*, 55.

the physical portal through which she came to the realization of her value.[56] Her story depicts the courage her mother gave her to see beyond what could be seen to the eternal truth of her divine ontology. Remembering the way her mother healed her from impetigo, Stubbs recounts,

> My mother always held prayer service as her hands washed my head and face. I was never certain of what she said; she talked under her breath. Between mumbles, she moaned old church hymns. Sometimes, though, in the midst of her mumbles and moans, I could hear the words, "Heal her. . . . Her steady intonations produced a sacred rhythm and the mere thought of disturbing her hallowed groove caused the sores on my head to sting."[57]

Stubbs describes HTT (Healing through Touch) as a holistic practice of healing that attends to the mind and spirit through the body. Identical to the choreography of erotic care of the soul, I argue the body serves as the locus of encounter for the healer, the wounded, and the divine. Through this erotic practice, Stubbs's mother attends to Stubbs's isness through a defiant appreciation for her daughter's body—a body deemed detestable/undesirable by the world's standards. Stubbs's mother conveys her love physically, affirming Stubbs's body as beloved and worthy of care, while exhibiting her own ability to harness the divine.

Stubbs's mother's touch was no ordinary touch; according to Stubbs, it held sacred significance. I maintain her mother's touch was the manifestation of love facilitated by flesh and a plea to the divine to use her erotic ritual as a conduit for spiritual intervention.[58] According to Stubbs, her mother's healing operated out of a very basic concept:

> The spiritual and mental effects of the illness had to be cured along with the physical symptoms. Healing had to reach the damaged spirit and mind—the side effects of the physical illness—or consequences as detrimental as the physical illness, if not more so could occur.[59]

Like Copeland and Wallace, Stubbs maintains that the erotic hospitality and care demonstrated through HTT are reminiscent of the erotic ministry of Jesus:

---

56 Monya Stubbs, "Be Healed: A Black Woman's Sermon on Healing through Touch," in Wade Gayles, *My Soul Is a Witness*, 305.

57 Stubbs, "Be Healed," 305–6.

58 Wardi, "A Laying On of Hands."

59 Stubbs, "Be Healed," 306.

When remembering my mother's insistence on touching me, I am reminded of biblical stories about the healing ministry of Jesus. . . . . Jesus often used touch as part of healing and restoring ill persons to health. Seldom did he merely speak deliverance without some form of physical contact."[60]

Stubbs distinguishes merely speaking deliverance and employing physical touch in healing psychological trauma and spiritual brokenness, arguing that the spoken word alone does not sufficiently attend to the spiritual and mental dimensions of illness.[61] Her mother's erotic acts of care, like the embodied spiritual care of Jesus, met Stubbs at the heart of her affliction. She refused to shun what the world deemed contaminated. Like Jesus, she shared the "space of sorrow" with her daughter—the place where her physical, psychic, and spiritual affliction met.[62] Incorporating these oft-neglected dimensions of healing, Stubbs's mother's erotic care illustrates how the spiritual and psychic are inextricably bound to our physical being. "The physical distortions of illness create a brokenness in one's self worth," Stubbs's mother contends.[63] However, I argue, through the power of touch—that is, through loving physical encounter with other bodies—the significance of one's body is transformed.

Stubbs's mother recognizes that stigmatizing assaults on the body impact the mind and the spirit as well. Since Stubbs's skin was the impetus of her classmates' rejection, it was vital that the shame inflicted upon her be dealt with at the source. Her mother's methods emphasize that Black women's healing requires a process that begins in the body and, through their innate connection, reaches into the psychological, social, and spiritual. Stubbs's mother's physio-spiritual attention to her daughter provides the kinds of life-giving sociality necessary for combating stigma. These experiences render Stubbs's body worthy and welcome, experiences integral to discovering self-love and reintegration. With this new sense data, Stubbs orients her sense of self in the affirming experiences of inclusion and renunciation that her mother's erotic relationality provides. In effect, her erotic care allows for Stubbs's transcendence from an identity rooted in shame and ridicule to one cultivated by a love that bests deleterious ideologies.

---

60 Stubbs, "Be Healed," 306–7.
61 Stubbs, "Be Healed," 307.
62 Stubbs, "Be Healed," 308.
63 Stubbs, "Be Healed," 307.

Erotic care of the soul, or HTT in Stubbs's case, declares, through radical acts of care and hospitality, what had been categorized as corrupt and obscene worthy of love and inclusion. Such encounters also have the power to transform the significance of the body by affording subjects of care experiences of their bodies as something other than a site of disease.

HTT as erotic care of the soul and erotic defiance "rejects social condemnation of the ill."[64] By touching those who are considered "unclean," healers reject the negative status of those afflicted with disease. Such practices exemplify the power of the erotic to challenge the notion that particular kinds of bodies, whether diseased or misfortunately gendered or raced, are unworthy, undesirable, and inappropriate for contact and connection. What Stubbs gestures at, but stops short of naming, is the capacity of erotic care/healing touch to provide alternative significance for one's flesh. Unfazed by the contagious nature of her disease, Stubbs's mother treats her infected skin without gloves. Through acts of sacrificial embodied hospitality, she puts her own health at risk to meet and welcome her daughter's body as cherished and beloved, with her own. When Stubbs asks her mother if she is concerned about contaminating herself, her mother responds, "Yes. But there is more at stake. . . . Your self-esteem is being shattered; your spirit is troubled. In order to heal you, I must touch you, I must feel you."[65] Stubbs's mother's insistence on uninhibited encounter extends beyond the physical. Her touch is fortified by love that seeks to reach beyond her daughter's skin into Stubbs's isness. In this way, their physical flesh serves as the locus of a psychic and spiritual encounter in which her mother's desire for Stubbs's holistic well-being reaches deeply into Stubbs's mind and spirit, challenging and rejecting the violence enacted upon her by her classmates with the truth of her body as beloved.

Of great importance is the intimacy of her mother's loving hands that, animated by her fervent prayer, facilitates corporeal conscientization, that is, awareness born out of the body's experience of the pleasure of "belovedness." Through this intimacy, the truth of the goodness and value of the body becomes a resource for resistance to the forces that daily malign and constrict Black female moral agency. Activating what womanist ethicist Stacey Floyd Thomas characterizes as redemptive self-love, the internal sense of worth and celebration of oneself necessary to overcome the imposition of inferiority

---

64 Stubbs, "Be Healed," 307.
65 Stubbs, "Be Healed," 306.

and wretchedness thrust upon Black women by racist patriarchy, corporeal conscientization foments a process of redemption and transformation.[66] Returning to Ciel's erotic baptism in Naylor's *The Women of Brewster Place*, Ciel is redeemed, reconciled, and resuscitated through Mattie's intimate washing of guilt and shame from her body. Imparting Ciel's belovedness, Mattie unashamedly attends to even the sexualized parts of Ciel's body with reverence.

Like heat thawing the frostbitten, returning life to numbed extremities, the experience of the erotic ignites vitality to the stifled hopes and desires of the dispossessed. As Black women become corporeally conscious of their belovedness, worth, sacrality, and power, the necessity for them to dissociate from their bodies in an attempt to guard themselves from disappointment, pain, and stigma is quieted, silenced by the pleasure of the body's validation, belonging, and connection. Ciel's corporeal conscientization facilitates reintegration of the dissociated parts of her personhood and resurrection of her once-dispossessed will. In Ciel's case, her reconciliation is signified by a moaning from deep within and tears that fall from her eyes and roll down into her lap and, ultimately, her pubic hair. Other accounts of erotic care depict those reintegrated by the erotic, resuscitated in will too—taking renewed responsibility for their lives. Stubbs, for instance, discovers her calling to holistic healing, ministering to the pain of others, as her mother ministered to her.[67] Such accounts give life to Lorde's assertion in "Uses of the Erotic: The Erotic as Power" when she writes, "For when we begin to recognize our deepest feelings, we begin to give up, of necessity being satisfied with suffering and self-negation. . . . In touch with the erotic, I become less willing to accept powerlessness . . . despair, depression, self-denial."[68] The erotic arouses resistance. Revitalized by the intensity of emotion and pleasure felt in the body, the dispossessed are inspired to defiance of all that seeks to constrain the fullness of their being.

Resistance is a function of the will. However, as previously explained, the legacy of dispossession can disintegrate Black subjectivity such that the will is bludgeoned into submission. The honoring of oneself, or self-love, however, gives way to radical subjectivity, the boldness of self-determination, which allows Black women to assert their identities on their own terms. Lorde's

---

66 For more, see Floyd-Thomas, *Mining the Motherlode.*
67 Stubbs, "Be Healed," 309.
68 Lorde, "Uses of the Erotic," 58.

"Uses of the Erotic" outlines the erotic's integral role in the construction of the conscientized agent. She contends that pleasure underscores an individual's capacity for joy, making her or him unwilling to settle for less, and therefore "responsible to" themselves.[69] Manifesting itself as a sense of fulfillment and desire (read: aspirations and yearning for connection and attainment) that moves the will, the seat of subjectivity to present and assert itself, erotic care, and I argue, the erotic in general, not only empowers the subject through a disclosure and awareness of her own desire but also imbues her with the capacity and the will to offer love to others. Reminiscent of Lorde's explication that eros is a transformative power, a creative force that makes it impossible for those who have participated in its pleasures to act out of a desire for their own and the freedom of others, Black women's literary tradition attests to the power of the erotic to mobilize Black women to responsibility.

In Alice Walker's *The Color Purple*, the protagonist Celie's bathing of the woman who should have been her nemesis, Shug Avery, provides an explicitly sexual example. Walker writes,

> First time I got the full sight of Shug Avery long black body with its black plum nipples, look like her mouth, I thought I had turned into a man. . . .
> What you staring at? She ast. Hateful. . . .
> You never seen a naked woman before . . . ?
> No ma'am, I said. I never did. . . .
> She say, Well take a good look, even if I is just a bag of bones now. She had the nerve to put one hand on her hip and bat her eyes at me. Then she suck her teef and roll her eyes at the ceiling while I wash her.
> I wash her body, it feel like I'm praying. My hands tremble and my breath short.[70]

Shug's posture is striking. Though sick, frail, and soaking wet, her body wields erotic power because of the confidence she has in its value. Despite its current infirmities, as her hand on her hip and her bat of her eyes suggest, she considers her body a gift—something special to behold. Shug, a woman who has known pleasure, has quite the reputation among the community as a "nasty woman."[71] Based on Lorde's theory of the erotic, however, Shug's embracing of sexual pleasure can be considered a good

---

69 Lorde, "Uses of the Erotic," 58.
70 Walker, *The Color Purple*, 49.
71 Walker, *The Color Purple*, 54.

thing, as it functions as a gateway to a greater sense of herself, her virtue, and her capacity for excellence.[72] Showcasing radical subjectivity, Shug is aware that her worth is not a product of what others say or think about her, but begins with her esteem for herself; she knows she must set the tone and others will follow her lead. Her erotic power is evinced by the impact she has on Celie.

Walker's depiction of Celie's erotic encounter with Shug presents the resurrection of emotion and will accomplished through experiences of desire, specifically Celie's for Shug. While the nature of Celie's desire is sexual in nature, Walker's expansive approach to the erotic reveals the ways sexual desire can transcend physical and social boundaries. Disregarding the traditional binaries that suggest that women must only be sexually attracted to men, as well as the boundaries that distinguish the self from the other, Walker depicts the ubiquity of the effect of erotic experiences on our being. As the story unfolds, Celie experiences an awakening, not only in her sexual organs, but also in her spiritual being. Her experience of sexual arousal feels like "praying," Celie says. Implying that washing Shug's body feels like connecting with the divine, Walker queers the sexual and the spiritual, refusing to limit them to one aspect of being. Additionally, Celie's attraction to Shug is about more than either woman's body; rather, Celie's desire is borne out of Shug's isness—the interstices of her confidence, her spirit, and her tenaciously guarded command of self. More than just her body, Celie desires to participate in Shug's *being* for herself. She does not simply want to be *like* Shug; she wants to *be* Shug. Her attraction exceeds epithymia—the desire to inhabit a sexual partner's body in the coital sense.[73] Her desire is beyond the physical, in that were it possible, Celie would wear Shug's body like a dress, taking up residence within her, that she might participate in Shug's self-determination and sass. It is Shug's posture in the world, *as well as* her "black plum nipples" and the desire they inspire, that regenerates Celie.[74] Shug brings her back to life by stirring in Celie the will to do more than survive, but to live.

Prior to her encounter with Shug, Celie's aim is simply to stay alive. Yet through Celie's discovery of desire for and connection with Shug—her

---

72 Lorde, "Uses of the Erotic," 88.
73 Baker-Fletcher, "The Erotic in Contemporary Black Women's Writings," 201.
74 Walker, *The Color Purple*, 49.

tending to her, nurturing her, and witnessing Shug's audacity to think something of herself, even in her weakest state—life is rekindled in Celie. Prior to her encounter with Shug, Celie functions more as an object of other people's whims as opposed to a person with a will of her own. Shug, however, reconnects Celie to her capacity for feeling, long crushed by the loss of her sister.[75] Shug's self-love, radical subjectivity, and sensuality are, for Celie, an invitation into the fullness of her own subjectivity. Such power is especially important to the oppressed because of bodily difference. As Spillers argues, the pornographic abuse of Blacks has alienated Black women from their capacity for feeling and agency in the world. The erotic in this case is depicted as a bridge that reconnects Celie with her desire and her will. Through the erotic's power of transcendence she moves from object to subject. After her erotic awakening, Celie takes on a willful, even defiant, posture. She speaks to her abuser, Mr., with greater authority and even engages in covert rebellion by spitting in Mr.'s father's water when he attempts to deprecate Shug.[76] Though his disparaging remarks about Shug are nothing new, Celie is. Her admiration and desire to participate in the love Shug has inside herself make Celie different. It ignites within her a desire to do more than exist but to fight.

Lorde's words bear repeating: "In touch with the erotic, [Celie became] less willing to accept powerlessness."[77] Through her example, Walker demonstrates how the erotic incites within us deep responsibility, the same kind of responsibility that renders Black women of the same ethical substance as Jesus, according to Marshall Turman—a responsibility that demands excellence of and for herself, as one who has experienced the depths of such fullness and satisfaction within. Cultural critic and Black feminist bell hooks suggests that for Black people satisfaction with and love for oneself threaten the social order. In her essay "Loving Blackness as Political Resistance," hooks contends that an attitude of love of and responsibility towards oneself, as a Black person, is suspect, dangerous, and threatening:[78]

> Collectively, black people and our allies in struggle are empowered when we practice self-love as a revolutionary intervention that undermines the practices

---

75 Lorde, "Uses of the Erotic," 57.

76 Walker, *The Color Purple*, 54–55.

77 Lorde, "Uses of the Erotic," 58.

78 bell hooks, *Black Looks: Race and Representation* (New York: Routledge, 1992), 20.

of domination. Loving blackness as political resistance transfers our ways of looking and being, and creates the conditions for us to move against the forces of domination and death and reclaim black life.[79]

The ability to love oneself, according to hooks, makes possible a radical shift in our experience of the world and ourselves, calling us into responsibility for the same. This responsibility recognizes the value of the self, though not in pursuit of aggrandizement or privilege, but within the context of the self in community with others, such that communal salvation rather than individual salvation is the telos of individual agents, illustrating again the power of the erotic to gather together disparate parts of a whole and resurrect that which seems dead.

As Ciel's, Stubbs's, Sethe's, and Celie's stories present, erotic care is intimate, explosive, disruptive, revelatory, and regenerative. These redemptive practices often require handling the most intimate parts of ourselves, parts we cannot shy away from out of fear, shame, or confusion about our bodies or the erotic. The inclusion of instances of the erotic in Black women's literature amplifies this truth, bringing to bear the restorative possibilities of erotic touch and its ability to affirm and validate Black women's existence in a world that thrives on their exploitation. Facilitating a kind of self and intracommunal determination regarding the bodies, identities, and agency of Black women, these experiences birth in women, perpetually degraded on account of their race, a corporal consciousness that they are vessels of divine power and worthy of love.

The erotic practice of bathing is a ritual of transformation in the literary work of Black women. Comparable to the waters of baptism, which evokes the Christian ritual of the death of the subject of care to the ways of the world and of the birth of new life in the Spirit of Christ, erotic care underscores Black women writers' perception of the power of the erotic to transform subjects from a degenerate state of being to a state of wholeness. Returning to *The Women of Brewster Place*, Mattie's acts of care serve as an external baptism for Ciel. However, the efficacy of her loving works is evinced in the internal baptism Ciel undergoes through her tears.

> Her tears no longer fried within her, killing her internal organs with their steam.

---

79 hooks, *Black Looks*, 20.

> So Ciel began to cry—there, naked, in the center of the bathroom floor. . . .
> The tears were flowing so freely now Ciel couldn't see, and she allowed herself to be led as if blind. She sat in the chair and cried—head erect. Since she made no effort to wipe them away, the tears dripped down her chin and landed on her chest and rolled down to her stomach and onto her dark pubic hair. . . .
> Ciel sat. And cried. The unmolested tears had rolled down her parted thighs and were beginning to wet the chair. But they were cold and good. She put out her tongue and began to drink their saltiness, feeding on them.[80]

Ciel's tears represent the reintegration of her personhood, the uniting of her body, once again with her feelings. Her situation is a reminder that the severing of one's desire and will from one's body is the principle characteristic of Black oppression. So devastated was Ciel by the horror of her circumstances, she had completely divorced herself from her feelings as a way to cope. However, Ciel's situation also communicates the power of the erotic to remedy this fracture. As Black women use the erotic capacities of their bodies to heal other Black women, they enact a love that unites body and spirit and resuscitates the will. Thus, erotic care, carried out by Black women, is more than just feel-good moments of loving touch. It is the revelatory power of God in flesh, calling Black women into consciousness of their power to persist and resist.

---

80 Naylor, *The Women of Brewster Place*, 104–5.

CHAPTER THREE

I Put a Spell on You

Conjuring Phantasms for Freedom

Erotic care of the soul is perhaps the most palatable version of erotic defiance for those squeamish about using the erotic as a religious category. By offering what I call corporeal conscientization, erotic care of the soul is the first step in Black women's emancipation from a dispossessed state and agential anemia and toward the formation of an erotically defiant agent. The practice, I have argued, offers Black women positive and pleasurable experiences of their flesh as beloved by the divine and a self-concept grounded in and affirmed by Black women's role in manifesting the love of God. These practices reconcile body, soul, and spirit, while clarifying the impact Black women have on each other's moral development.

While the erotic defiance of erotic care of the soul operates in the private spaces of Black women's intimate communities, the erotic defiance of the self-possessed and self-determined Black female agent is far more transgressive. She is self-authorized. She maintains control of her body and sexuality. She unabashedly asserts her cultural allegiance and revels in the distinctiveness of Black women's embodiment. Not only does the erotically defiant Black female agent resist domination at the hands of men, institutions, and Western hegemony, but she contests these powers for the world to see. Her practice of Black womanhood provokes change through an embodied praxis of resistance, self-definition, and world-making that audaciously asserts self-possession and freedom through her body and sexuality.

In my classroom, when I ask my students to offer examples of sexually self-possessed Black women, the names of hip-hop and R&B provocateurs like

Nicki Minaj, Beyoncé, Rihanna, and newcomers like Lizzo and Megan Thee Stallion are often at the top of the list. Musical hybrids who dance double-dutch on the lines that separate rap emcees and songstresses, these artists operate as signifiers and change makers as they defiantly assert their agency through the celebration of Black and female sexual power. In this chapter I take up the performances, practices, and postures of these cultural icons, who I call Provocatrixters. More of an idea or archetype than a characterization of any particular artist, the Provocatrixter is driving influence in the American cultural ethos. She is a cultural performer who operates as a conjuror of sorts, calling forth a version of Black womanhood through performances and postures of sexual-gender transgression that challenges the hegemonic imagination and its monolithic values.[1]

Operating in the conjurational tradition Thee Smith presents in *Conjuring Culture*, the Provocatrixter's artistry can be likened to the preacher's embodiment of "the presence of the God he preached."[2] Having perfected the art of compelling our participation, she beguiles us, seducing us, as Audre Lorde has argued, not simply in the doing, but in the depth of feeling in which she acts. Present in the seductive energy of Beyoncé's and Missy's 2013 and 2015 Super Bowl spell-binding performances, or Jill Scott's or Erykah Badu's command of themselves, the stage, and their audience when they perform live, the life-affirming power they exude conjures a powerful version of Black womanhood into material reality.

Leveraging their bodies as signifiers in the world, they in some instances act as catalysts for the practice of self-authorization in their Black female audiences who emulate and mimic performances of sexual-gender transgression through what I call corporeal incantation. Yet not all performances are equal. While many would equate all transgressive performances of the Provocatrixter with erotic defiance, this chapter aims to clarify important distinctions between the sexual chords of erotic resistance and commodified sexual spectacle, and to discern what aspects of these performances prove beneficial to Black women's liberation and what aspects are potential detriments.

Women's sexuality is often depicted as a kind of charm, power, or influence used to manipulate their worlds. Within the Christian tradition, this power is framed as sinister, dangerous, and detrimental. It is antithetical to

---

1 Theophus Smith, *Conjuring Culture: Biblical Formations of Black America* (New York: Oxford University Press, 1994), 23.

2 Smith, *Conjuring Culture*, 23.

God and framed by church father Augustine as concupiscence.[3] Part of a pantheon of debilitating passions that prevent humans from the good—the rational and the godly—sexual desire, according to Augustine—let alone the flexing of sexual power—threatened the spiritual health of those who did not suppress such urges.[4] Those who did capitalize on the power of desire enacted their wills in rebellion to God's will and were therefore separated from God. However, womanist and feminist theologians take a different view. Rather than antithetical to the divine, they consider human sexuality part of the very image of the divine. Womanist practitioners like Margaret Walker Alexander describe human sexuality as deeply connected to spirituality, allowing Black women to more deeply connect to God within. More than just the body, human sexuality encompasses one's spiritual self and connects humans to the divine within.[5] Often spiritual power of Black women's sexualities and the erotic nature of their spiritualities, are understood as a form of magic that allows them to manipulate the world for good and for evil.

The term *magic* is not happenstance. Given the misanthropy with which women's, especially Black women's, bodies and their powers are perceived, it is unsurprising that the power of Black women's sexuality would be categorized as part of the occult. Historian Yvonne Chireau's definition of magic as "the religion of the other" and "a particular approach or attitude by which humans interact with unseen powers or spiritual forces" however, offers a more contextual religious lens. For Black women's sexual power/agency is often used as a curative solution to oppression and the various circumstances in which Black people felt and feel powerless, in much the way Black people used the contested religious category of conjure.[6] In fact, many Black women through history until this very day have used their sexual power as a way of reclaiming their authority over their bodyselves, thereby conjuring a better life and a better world.

Framing Black women's sexual power in the tradition of conjure, I want to underscore the unique context of exploitation and (un)freedom, out of which Black women's sexual power is often exercised as a way of resisting

---

3 Augustine, *City of God*, c.xxvi.

4 Augustine, "On the Good of Marriage," trans. Charles Wilcox (Maryknoll, NY: Catholic University of America Press, 1955), bk. 8:19–21. See also Mark Jordan, *The Ethics of Sex* (Oxford: Blackwell Publishers, 2002), 109.

5 Buckner, "Spirituality, Sexuality and Creativity," 226.

6 Yvvonne Chireau, *Black Magic: Religion and the African American Conjuring Tradition* (Berkeley: University of California Press, 2003), 3.

what Edward Phillip Antonio calls facile celebrations. Facile celebrations are strategies of reclamation that attempt to disconnect historical pain from the use and abuse of Black bodies.[7] Celebration of Black women's sexuality and its practice is a principal element of the Provocatrixter's power to conjure a self-possessed, self-directed Black womanhood; however, it is important to remember that this power is always circumscribed by racist patriarchal domination and capitalism. These factors, I argue, commodify, exploit, and deform practices intended for liberation into performances of the pornographic. Erotic defiance, on the other hand (and the liberated agency it represents), I contend, is the basis of a womanist ethic of freedom. Its practice offers ways of being that both unburden Black women from facile celebrations of the erotic and empower the possibilities, responsibilities, and power of erotic self-determination.

THE CONJURING POWER OF BLACK WOMEN'S SEXUALITY

In his book *Conjuring Culture*, Thee Smith describes conjure as an African-based form of magic and a tradition of healing and harming that "transforms reality through performances and processes involving a mimetic use of medicinal and toxic substances."[8] Mapping and manipulating the world through signs, symbols, and symbolic phenomena, conjure he argues, is an enduring form of ritual speech and action, "intended to perform what it expresses."[9] Stories of conjure, canonized in African American cultural expression like folktales, literature, and the blues, depict men and women soliciting the assistance of a conjure woman or hoodoo doctor to assist them in negotiating challenges they did not have the material resources to overcome, including sick family members with no access to medical care, defense against masters with penchants for violence, and, of course, the attention of philandering lovers who seemed incapable of fidelity.

Conjure was magic for those disempowered by racism and patriarchy. It offered one of few avenues of recourse in circumstances that seemed

---

7 Edward Phillip Antonio, "Desiring Booty and Killing the Body: Toward Negative Erotics," in Pinn and Hopkins, *Loving the Body*, 272.

8 Smith, *Conjuring Culture*, 31.

9 Smith, *Conjuring Culture*, 4.

insurmountable. Situating African conjurational spirituality in Christian terms, Smith emphasizes the validity of conjure as a spiritual methodology of agency and a prominent organizing feature in all Black religious experiences, from Black diasporic religions such as the voudou practiced in the Caribbean islands, to Candomblé in Brazil, Santeria in the Spanish-speaking Americas, and even in Black Christianity practiced in the United States.[10] For example, Christian practices of invoking divine power through ritually patterned behaviors like the performative use of language and symbols—what Western society perceives as heathen behavior—is described by Smith as an alternative expression of an identical desire for supernatural assistance. Even behaviors like obedience and the practice of righteousness, he argues, have "conjurational intent," in that African American Christians use them to invoke divine help from a liberating God in the same way practitioners of conjure deploy incantations and the pharmacopeia of conjure.[11] While conjurational practices exist in traditional forms of religion, Smith extends conjure's reach to the various cultural performances that make up Black expressive culture.[12]

Approaching the Provocatrixter from Smith's perspective, I underscore the performances of Provocatrixters as intrinsically conjurational, mediating an African worldview within Black American interpretation of its Western contexts and communicating and performing Black Americans' intentions for sociohistorical transformation.[13] Accordingly these performances have a ritual effect. They even serve as a form of religiosity, for the women and girls who participate in the music and images. Sexual conjure, for the Provocatrixter of contemporary Black music, begins with the reclamation of their bodies from the powerlessness of dispossession. Through their music and example, they help their majority Black female audiences do the same. Mimicking their postures, Black women participate in the manifestation of the will through the bodily choreography of participants, such that their understandings of themselves and their world are transformed in much the same way hymns and worship experiences allow churchgoers to be made over. Integral to my argument is Smith's emphasis on the discursive properties of magic and conjure as a special mode of signification, a way of contributing meaning in the world. As Smith attests, magic is a way of managing the world in the form of

---

10 Smith, *Conjuring Culture*, 3–6.
11 Smith, *Conjuring Culture*, 22.
12 Smith, *Conjuring Culture*, 6, 137.
13 Smith, *Conjuring Culture*, 4, 6, 14, 57.

signs. It is, in fact, a language system constructed to manipulate the world, or in the case of the Provocatrixter, worldviews, through ritual speech and action intended to perform what it expresses through the crafting of signs that embody the inner power of the will.[14]

The same kind of mapping accomplished by the magic of conjure, I argue, is operative through Western hegemony's construction of the discursive (signified) Black body. Exercising the will of Western white subjects over Black existence, pornographic caricatures of Blackness conjured in the white immoral imagination exalt themselves above the divine design of the *imago Dei* in Black being. Animating obscene rituals of impoverishment, neglect, and denigration of Black flesh, these caricatures overdetermine Black women's identities and incite violence against them.

In their attempts to loosen hegemony's grip on their lives, Black women from clubwomen to blues women have leveraged the politization of their bodies and sexualities for subversion. The Provocatrixter is no different; "gaining insurgent ground for black women as female social subjects," to use the words of Hortense Spillers, the Provocatrixter deploys sexuality homeopathically per the tradition of conjure as a way of naming and narrating the world as she sees it.[15] Her version of the story grows out of the distinct circumstances of Black women's situation, specifically the sexual politics that dictate how her body is read and the limited choices available to her to liberate herself from the cage of Western significations. Conjuring a version of Black womanhood in the traditions of Black clubwomen and blues women, the Provocatrixter combines her artistry, the power of her sexuality, and fidelity to Black culture to call into being a greater range of freedom from which to operate.[16]

Fidelity to Black culture is a principal quality of African American conjurors. Conjure represented a spiritual resource drawn from the distinctive

---

14 Smith, *Conjuring Culture*, 4.

15 Writing about the problematizing of gender in the lives of Black women, Spillers avers that more important to the well-being of Black women than becoming a part of the cult of true womanhood is a radical subjectivity, which gives her the power to name and narrate the world as she sees it. For more, see Spillers, "Mama's Baby, Papa's Maybe," 80.

16 It is crucial to remember that Black women's attempts at liberation according to Katie Cannon will always result in "a greater range of freedom" rather than freedom itself, "due to the extraneous forces and the entrenched bulwark of white supremacy and male superiority which pervades this society." As a result, Black women and men are forced to live with different ranges of freedom. For more, see Cannon, *Black Womanist Ethics*, 3.

power of their Africanity and their authentic spiritual selves; thus their participation in the art conveyed their allegiance to and confidence in a Black and African cultural and cosmological framework that stood over and against Western conceptions of divine power.[17] Continuing in this tradition, Provocatrixters, despite their influence in the dominant culture, choose to operate in the subaltern, affirming the moral philosophies and aesthetic values of Black communities as the prevailing standard of their lives. Their loyalty to a Black subaltern culture in turn makes them more powerful, as their influence in popular culture is mediated by their ability to inspire desire in their audience, the desire to look, touch, and taste the taboo energy of Black female sexuality and potentially be manipulated by it.

In addition to her fidelity to the taboo world of Blackness, the Provocatrixter's authority is constructed by her sexual acumen. In "The Arts of Loving," Lisa Gail Collins explains that conjurors' authority was rooted in their knowledge of how to influence and direct spiritual forces, especially in an effort to manipulate desire for power and control.[18] This they accomplished through objects like the mojo arm of conjure and other elements of the earth that represented both romance and the object of their magic. These elements provided the *materia medica*[19] effective in activating spiritual forces that made trifling lovers who mistreat their women behave. In addition to their charm bag, conjurors' physical bodies evoked love, desire, passion, and power to change the ethical course of individuals and systems. Employing forms of seductive subversion as magic to put a spell on or spiritually control those who constrain her agency in the world, many a desperate woman has dramatically changed the course of her life. Accordingly, sexual power as conjure functions as a means of survival, or what Thee Smith calls a "curative transformation of [her] reality."[20]

---

17 Kameelah Martin, "Conjuring Moments and Other Such Hoodoo: African American Women and Spirit Work" (PhD diss., Florida State University, 2006), 140.

18 Lisa Gail Collins, "The Art of Loving," in *Women and Religion in the African Diaspora: Knowledge, Power, and Performance,* ed. R. Marie Griffith and Barbara Dianne Savage (Baltimore: Johns Hopkins University Press, 2006), 199.

19 Smith, *Conjuring Culture,* 5, 31.

20 Smith, *Conjuring Culture,* 5.

SEDUCTION AS AN ETHICAL CURE

To the Christian reader, the manipulation of desire treads dangerously toward the sin of exploitation. However, acts of seduction are present throughout the Bible, from Genesis to Revelation. The biblical stories of Ruth and Esther, especially, offer scenarios in which the power of seduction is deployed for the purposes of God. After her first husband's death, Ruth, a Moabite woman under the tutelage of her mother-in-law Naomi, intentionally uses her sexuality to lure her kinsman, Boaz, into assuming responsibility for their survival. Flexing her feminine charms, Ruth presents herself as a damsel in distress while gleaning from the harvest of Boaz's fields, hoping he will "take notice."[21] When he happens upon her, Boaz finds favor with Ruth, such that he immediately starts taking responsibility for her needs, instructing his employees to not only allow her to glean, but to glean beyond the corners mandated by Levitical law.[22] In fact, Boaz provides for Ruth with such generosity, that Ruth's needs are met in his presence and in his absence. For when she returns home to Naomi she has collected so much food that both she and her mother-in-law are provided for.

Some scholars suggest that Naomi, wanting to secure Boaz's provision permanently, instructs Ruth to set a sexual trap. Biblical scholar Edward F. Campbell suggests that it is Naomi's intention for Ruth to make herself "enticing" and "irresistible" in the sexual sense.[23] Further she encourages Ruth to slip onto the threshing floor, a place some scholars argue was known for its revelry and sex, and "uncover his feet" after Boaz is full and drunk with wine.[24] Biblical scholars note that the frequent use of the term *feet* is a euphemism for men's genitals and cite this passage as a narrative of sex for payment. Yet the language is ambiguous. The deletion of verse 9 from the ancient Syriac versions of the Bible and the Targum, however, offers further

---

21 Ruth 2:19, author's paraphrase.

22 From the Hebrew word *laqat*, which means "to pick or gather." Gleaning was a Hebrew practice commanded by law, which dictated that land owners were to refrain from harvesting the corners of a field so that they could be left for the poor, widows, orphans, and strangers, i.e., foreigners. For more, see Deuteronomy 24:21 and Jennifer L. Koosed, *Gleaning Ruth: A Biblical Heroine and Her Afterlives* (Columbia: University of South Carolina Press, 2001).

23 Edward F. Campbell, *Ruth: A New Translation with Introduction, Notes, and Commentary* (New Haven, CT: Yale University Press, 2011).

24 Schadrac Keita and Janet Dyk, "The Scene at the Threshing Floor: Suggestive Readings and Intercultural Considerations on Ruth 3," *The Bible Translator* 57 (2006): 17–32.

credence to the idea that the passage contains sexual allusions, such that the verse had to be censored for religiously respectable readers.[25] This evidence, coupled with the translation of "uncovered" as Ruth uncovering her own nakedness, or more salaciously Ruth uncovering the genitals of Boaz, lends itself to a sexually loaded interpretation in which Ruth performs oral sex on Boaz hoping to find favor, not only for her survival and that of her mother-in-law, but in accordance with the will of God such that she becomes part of the lineage of Jesus.[26] Though Ruth was not mandated by God to seduce Boaz, her actions are efficacious in making way for the will and desires of God, calling into question the veracity of God's condemnation of women's sexual agency. Similarly, Queen Esther's powers of sexual seduction during her night with King Xerxes position her to become queen of Persia, enabling her to lead the Jewish people in a spiritual fast that saves them from the evil machinations of the king's adviser, Haman. Repeatedly, the text offers the words, "For such a time as this," suggesting that the impending doom of God's chosen people justified a mediating ethic of sexuality that preempted the purity codes of Jewish law.

While the examples of Ruth and Esther offer evidence of the divine use of seduction in human action, the prophets Hosea and Jeremiah depict God, God's self, as seductive. In Hosea 2:14, God says, "Therefore, I will now allure her, and bring her into the wilderness, and speak tenderly to her." The tone of this conversation takes on romantic persuasion, as a lover would woo their love back after a conflict.[27] God's romantic affection is offered to Israel as it faces the possibility of a wilderness of captivity in Assyria. In this case, to allure is to entice, to offer a taste of God's goodness such that the people of Israel would desire to return to right relationship with God. By offering a snapshot of the seductive quality of God's love for God's wayward children, the reader sees God provoke human desire to lead God's people away from a life of sin. In an ecstatic climax of submission, Jeremiah proclaims the absolute irresistibility of God, calling out to the Lord, "O LORD, you have enticed me,

---

25 Keita and Dyk, "The Scene at the Threshing Floor," 20.

26 Many biblical scholars have argued that in Boaz's slumbering state, Ruth uncovers his "feet," a euphemism for his genitals. Many have suggested that Ruth and Boaz had a sexual encounter on the threshing floor, motivating Boaz to take Ruth as his bride to preserve her reputation, as well as his own. For more, see Judy Fentress Williams, *Ruth, Abingdon Old Testament Commentaries* (Nashville: Abingdon, 2012).

27 Joseph Benson, *Commentary of the Old and New Testaments* (New York: Carton and J. Porter, 1857).

and I was enticed; you have overpowered me" (Jer 20:7). In the economy of the God of Christianity, a victorious act of seduction overpowers its object, not with violence, but with a desire to know and be known. Accomplishing a change of mind and ethical course, often beyond an individual's ability to resist, yet contrary to the witness of the church, these seductive acts are congruent with the holiness and righteousness of God.

Beyond the erotic valences of the biblical text, the seductive power of the Provocatrixter echoes the magnetic and transformational force present in the Black preacher. James Weldon Johnson's account of his encounter with the preacher who inspired his poem "The Creation" offers insight. Johnson describes himself as a reluctant participant, uninterested in involving himself in the frenzy associated with Black church worship expressions. However, he too becomes swept up in the undercurrent of the energy of the preacher's performance. Not only did the power of the preacher's performance compel him to join in, its impact later inspired him to craft the poem "The Creation." In *Conjuring Culture*, Smith uses Johnson's account to offer a theopoetic analysis of the mimetic aspects of Black cultural performances to radically transform Euro-American ideologies for the consumption and philosophical aims of Black communities. However, his attention to Johnson's words regarding "the art by which the preacher was able to evoke through dramatic performance, the embodied presence of the God he preached" provides a relevant launching point for my theorization of erotic conjure as the practice of connecting to and acting as conduit of the Holy.[28]

The arts and powers of the preacher are emblematic of seduction as conjure and the praxis of meaning making in the world. I aver that the seduction of conjure consists of the power of corporeal performances as incantations, used to call forth, draw in, and transform reality. I use the language of incantation to convey the role of the body's movement in producing or invoking a particular spirit. Johnson describes the performativity of the preacher, his body language, his use of voice, his rocking back and forth, and even his moaning as a catalyst for a "compelling force" that fascinates, deeply moves, and evokes an irresistible emotional effect.[29] The preacher's bodily performance is creative. It generates the power to invoke or call forth the desire to know and participate in the power the performer embodies. It serves as the material out of which flows something not like this world, something that dances with

---

28 Smith, *Conjuring Culture*, 23.
29 Smith, *Conjuring Culture*, 23.

God in erotic celebration of union and embodied relationship.[30] Operating as transmitter, in a dance of flesh and spirit that operates in perichoretic symbiosis, the preacher provides the material substance, acting as a conduit for the delivery of divine energy into material reality in the form of performances of the divine, intelligible to human senses. His performance registers to the audience as something extraordinarily other, making accessible spiritual energy that inspires change. Such performances, I argue, whether issuing from the preacher or any cultural performer, equate to a kind of erotic artistry, a sacred collaboration of flesh and spirit. As a function of the performer's artistic gifts, these charisms mediate the creative, curative, and transformative power of the erotic, which registers in the affective—the production of emotion and desire.

REPRESENTATION AND THE ART OF MEANING MAKING

Artistry, like sexuality, is a spiritual capacity made possible by the creative, life-giving energy of the flesh. Leveraging her body and sexuality similarly to the way a witch doctor uses their conjuring instruments to communicate, interpret, understand, and shape the physical and spiritual world, the Provocatrixter taps into the sacred power of her body to create and construct meaning for the transformation of her reality.[31] Her performances have the capacity to invoke and direct the erotic as a spiritual resource for manipulating the symbols erected by racist, patriarchal hegemony, helping Black women come to terms with their ultimate significance and place in the world.[32] More than a master at her artistry, the Provocatrixter as conjuror in the tradition of Thee Smith is a master at the art of signification. Crafting her body as a sign and living symbol, her activity in the world contests, reifies, and remixes the values of the Western moral imagination through a sexually autonomous version of Black womanhood uniquely her own. In this way, she leverages the political significance of her body in the tradition of representation like clubwomen and blues women of the early twentieth century, offering alternative

---

30 Smith, *Conjuring Culture*, 23.

31 Smith, *Conjuring Culture*, 4.

32 Theologian Charles Long's definition contends, "The church is not the only context for the meaning of religion." For Long, religion signifies the processes by which an individual orients oneself and finds one's place in the world. Long, *Significations*, 7, via Chireau, *Black Magic*, 14.

meanings for Black womanhood that upend the assigned values of Black female flesh in the social imagination.

In quiet protest to the denial of Black humanity, Black women's exclusion from the cult of true womanhood, and the existential confinement such beliefs construct, Black clubwomen reached beyond class boundaries to educate recent Black female migrants in presentation, style, hair care, and other compulsory aesthetic and social practices in white, often city life. Heavily influenced by Eurocentric formulations of femininity, morality, and civility themselves, and guided by an ethic of sexual purity and sacrifice, clubwomen ascribed to these characteristics a religious symbolism, distinctive forms of holiness, congruent with Black women's invention of themselves as holy vessels for God's use.[33] As such, Black women sought additional safety and status through respectability and crafted in themselves an image of sexual modesty, taking great care to mute any aspects of desire within themselves that might inadvertently call attention to itself.[34] Their strategy elevated the image of Black people at large as moral and upright citizens in the white moral imagination while contributing to the survival and potential flourishing of poorer Black women.

Despite their well-meaning intentions, clubwomen's socioreligiously inspired strategies inadvertently contributed to Black women's self-erasure, or at least the erasure of their bodies for the benefit of social progress. Unwittingly exacting horizontal violence, these strategies, while presenting Black women as palatable, reinforced the white perception that Black women's sexuality has a corrosive impact on Black women's morality. Thus, Black women vying for respectability had to choose between the expression of essential aspects of their identity and the benefits that came with being considered worthy of dignity and respect.

---

33 Kelly Brown Douglas describes the "blasphemous body denying and body phobic sanctified narrative of civility." For more, see Douglas, *Black Bodies and the Black Church: A Blues Slant* (New York: Palgrave Macmillan, 2012), 181–82.

34 Historian Evelyn Higginbotham asserts that more than "mindless mimicry of white behavior," respectability has historically been used in a variety of ways. In the context of the Black clubwoman and the politics of respectability, a term coined by Higginbotham, respectability is the feeling an individual has when others find worth and value in them and treat them as such, procured through self-respecting, professional representation strategies. For more on the politics of respectability, see Higginbotham, *Righteous Discontent: The Women's Movement in the Black Baptist Church, 1880–1920* (London: Harvard University Press, 1993), 185–229.

In contrast, blues women, like Alberta Hunter, Ma Rainey, and Bessie Smith, defiantly contested the gender- and race-based limitations imposed upon Black women in the early twentieth century. They cultivated a version of Black womanhood directed by a drastically divergent moral philosophy, more akin to the Provocatrixter than the respectable Black lady. Blues women and those who emulated their way of life understood the power of their bodies and sexualities and wielded said power in ways that drastically differed from traditional sexual-gender norms of Christianity. In their moral universe, bodies and the desires that sprang from them were not burdens of evil that required hiding, but gifts—dynamic resources—that enabled them not only to survive, but to thrive through the money such performances garnered and the independence they made possible.

Consequently, blues women experienced and articulated a freedom in their sexualities that made space for Black women's multidimensionality, allowing them to exist in their fullness as sexual and spiritual beings. They unapologetically, in the many colors that expressed their inner being, were unbothered by the perceptions respectable society (both white and Black) may have held regarding their appearance, morality, or humanity. This sense of dignity and grace, cultivated within rather than without, empowered blues women to exhibit in the face of demonization and rejection unflinching self-pride, which served as a bulwark against white supremacist antipathy. Rather than chase after white society to prove their worth through clean work, clean habits, and respectable images, blues women declared themselves inherently worthy, rebuffing societal demands of respectability and defying the policing of their bodies. They were committed to living into what Emilie Townes calls their *isness*, in whole, not in part, such that the lives they lived were a repudiation of the domestication for which clubwomen clamored so desperately. For blues women, self-actualization was a life of freedom that required an unyielding self-love and a dogged commitment to self-determination.

Following in the example of clubwomen and blues women, Provocatrixters' bodies represent a fundamental source of their power to provoke change through the remixing of meaning. Serving as the site of contestation in the resistance of domination, Black female sexuality becomes the canvas for images of self-possession crafted through the transgression of sexual-gender and racial boundaries. Self-possession, after all, is a quintessential aspect of freedom in an existence steeped in bodily dispossession. A fundamental facet of what Western frameworks conceive as an ethical being, self-possession undergirds freedom. The slave, however, was never intended to be free. Similarly, the weight of capitalism, sexism, and racism have never allowed Black women to live lives beyond economic, political, and social desperation.[35] While Western concepts of moral agency assume the freedom to act in the world, such freedom has often eluded Black American women due to chattel slavery's influence on the social standing of Black women in America, and to patriarchy's subordination of women under the rule and control of men.

THE SIGNIFICANCE OF SEX

At the crux of Black women's moral agency is the issue of corporeal freedom, which within an Aristotelian schema is agential power. Moral agency in the Western ethical tradition is typically described as the ability to make reasonable judgments in pursuit of the good and be held accountable for the choices said judgments inspire. The normative moral agent, based on the evolution and trajectory of Western moral philosophies from Aristotle to Kant, is a rational soul who is self-directed and aims their actions toward the pursuit of the good, whether that be happiness, obedience to God, or the maturity of self-legislation. Their agency is predicated on their capacity for reason and the freedom to act deliberatively and voluntarily. Such freedom has eluded Black American women. Thus, the quest for agential freedom

---

35 "Single Black women household heads with a college degree have 38 percent less wealth ($5,000) than single white women without one ($8,000). Among married women who are the head of the household, Black women with a bachelor's degree have 79 percent less wealth ($45,000) than white women with no degree ($117,200) and 83 percent less wealth than those with one ($260,000). Marital status and education do not close the gap. On top of this, Black women also have greater student loan debt than Black men, white men, and white women. In 2016, the typical Black woman heading a household had $0 in home equity. And white women had nearly 10 times the value of stocks and bonds as Black women. These factors contribute to the lack of wealth among older Black women as they approach retirement. Similarly, Black women earn less than white people, despite educational attainment. For example, Black women without a high school diploma earn 61 percent of the median white men's wages, those with a bachelor's degree earn 64 percent, and those with more than a bachelor's degree earn just 60 percent." Taken from Justyce Watson and Ofronama Biu, "You Can't Improve Black Women's Economic Well-Being without Addressing Both Wealth and Income Gaps," Urban Institute, July 1, 2022: https://www.urban.org/urban-wire/you-cant-improve-black-womens-economic-well-being-without-addressing-both-wealth-and. For more, see Khaing Zaw, Jhumpa Bhattacharya, Anne Price, Darrick Hamilton, and William Darity Jr., "Women, Race & Wealth," *Research Brief Series* 1 (2017): https://www.insightcced.org/wp-content/uploads/2017/01/January2017_ResearchBriefSeries_WomenRaceWealth-Volume1-Pages-1.pdf.

for Black women begins by reclaiming their bodies and their ability to self-authorize. The Provocatrixter leads the way through sexual assertions of bodily autonomy and self-determination, a chief ethical principle by which Black women resist oppression.

Hip-hop pioneers Salt-N-Pepa reclaim their bodies by "shaking their thang." Missy Elliott declares her body as her own by playing the sexual initiator as she sings "Sock It 2 Me." Megan Thee Stallion asserts her power through her sexual acumen in "Savage." Through performances of sexual spectacle, Provocatrixters declare their freedom and agency. Perceived as mere vulgarity by outsiders, expressions of sexual desire, expertise, and pleasure in Black music like the blues have historically functioned as metaphors for existential freedom and a signifier for Black humanity, "covertly speaking back to the denial of Black men's masculinity and humanity in white society."[36] Blues women declared their humanity by celebrating its multidimensionality through their exhibition of desire and pleasure. However, rather than playing to the white gaze, this declaration sought to tap into the emancipatory power sexuality afforded them. Bawdy and unapologetic, this version of Black womanhood emancipated many singers from the limitations of gender that rendered many Black women dependent on men and jobs in domestic labor for financial security. The money earned through singing allowed them to live the life they sang about, a life that was governed by their wills and desires rather than the drudgery of subordination and service to men and white people.

Crafted in in the vein of their blues antecedents, the Provocatrixter's performance of sexuality emancipates her from the confines not only of gender, but of respectability and the dominion of Western aesthetics. Characterized by feistiness and aggressiveness necessitated by constant threats to Black women's physical, spiritual, and mental well-being, the Provocatrixter mimics an ethic of domination deeply embedded into every paradigm of power in the Western world. These gendered conceptions of dominance attribute power to the male by divine right, while the female is coded as subordinate and vulnerable because of her ability to be penetrated.[37] Attributed in part to the hegemony of the communities from which hip-hop is birthed, the masculinist ethos of hip-hop has deep roots in both the religious and social

---

36 James Cone, *The Cross and the Lynching Tree* (Maryknoll, NY: Orbis, 2011), 16.

37 Juan Floyd-Thomas, "A Jihad of Words: The Evolution of African American Islam and Contemporary Hip Hop," in *Noise and Spirit: The Religious Sensibilities of Rap Music*, ed. Anthony Pinn (New York: NYU Press, 2003).

orientations of the Black community. The Nation of Islam and Five Percenters, for instance, are a key influence within the earliest evolution of hip-hop music, and espouse an ideology of gender from a religious perspective that deifies men as gods and subordinates women, calling them earths. As gods, men have a responsibility to protect women as well as the right to rule over them.[38] These roles fortify Black male subjectivity and Black men's right to lead and control their own domain. These beliefs are the foundations of the counternarrative that challenges the inferiority of Black men and imbues them with power often denied by society.

The influence of the Black church and Christian theological anthropology is also significant. From the perspective of dominant interpretations of Christian Scripture, women are never to have any authority over a man, but must remain submissive, pure, and voiceless in sacred spaces. Further, as womanist ethicist Marcia Riggs notes, no room is given for femininity in the Godhead (Christianity's prevailing concept of divine power).[39] While more progressive Christian spaces make room for the possibility of feminine energy in the Holy Spirit, many Black churches continue to insist on referring to the Holy Spirit as "he."[40] In what cultural anthropologist Zora Neale Hurston describes as featherbed resistance, Provocatrixters' performance of sexual authority turns the dynamics of gender on their ear. "Featherbed resistance," states Hurston, patronizes *white curiosity*,

> that is, we let the probe enter, but it never comes out. It gets smothered under a lot of laughter and pleasantries. The theory behind our tactics: "The white man is always trying to know into somebody else's business. All right, I'll set something outside the door of my mind for him to play with and handle. He can read my writing but he sho' can't read my mind. I'll put this play toy in his hand, and he will seize it and go away. Then I'll say my say and sing my song."[41]

Similarly, Provocatrixters employ featherbed resistance to distract or lead men away from violence against them by beckoning audiences into a subaltern

---

38 Juan Floyd-Thomas, "A Jihad of Words."

39 Marcia Riggs, *Plenty Good Room: Women versus Male Power in the Black Church* (Cleveland: Pilgrim, 2003).

40 Wallace Best, "The Spirit of the Holy Ghost Is a Male Spirit: African-American Preaching Women and the Paradoxes of Gender," in Griffith and Savage, *Women and Religion in the African Diaspora*, 113.

41 Zora Neal Hurston, *Mules and Men* (Philadelphia: Lippincott, 1935; repr., New York: Collier, 1970), 1.

world made by their own sexuality. Mastered by hip-hop's prevailing Provo-catrixter, Nicki Minaj, in a teddy and lace thong in the 2012 video "Monster," the amplification of sexual desirability seeks to attract those driven by the traditional conceptions of desirability as virtue. Putting on theatric sexuality, as one would a costume, Minaj dangles her sexuality as "play toy" while guarding access to her personhood. Giving a nod to the notion of dissemblance,[42] she denies access to her reality—subverting by her featherbed resistance those who wish to oppress and subjugate. The genius of the strategy is that much like whites attempting to engage Blacks, those who engage Minaj, because of this ruse, believe themselves to have apprehended the fullness of her existence, when in reality, they have been imprisoned and subjugated by their own imaginations. Distracted, and in many ways consumed, by Minaj's sexual power, male dominance is inoculated, and she is given the space to freely determine how her sexuality will be deployed and when.

For example, Minaj's "Motorsport" both celebrates her sexual agency and heightens her sexual defiance.[43] With a salacious expression referring to the vagina's ability to self-lubricate when aroused, Minaj articulates active sexual desire and her willingness and freedom to express it in crude terms that transgress the boundaries of respectable womanhood. Deploying language often considered masculine, Minaj also degenders herself as a means of escaping the limitations and vulnerability of femininity. Though Minaj is one of the most overtly sexually transgressive, this same reconceptualization of female sexuality from passive and pious to active and provocative is a dominant theme in the Provocatrixter's vernacular. On the basis of the same biological signs of arousal described by Minaj, Missy Elliott boasts of her sexual superiority over other women in her song "I'm Better."[44] Through this linguistic device aided by innovatively sensual choreography Missy pushes against normative

---

42 Darlene Clarke Hine, "Rape and the Inner Lives of Black Women in the Middle West," in "Common Grounds and Crossroads: Race, Ethnicity, and Class in Women's Lives," special issue, *Signs* 14, no. 4 (Summer 1989): 912–20. Investigating Black club-women's histories in Detroit, Michigan, Hine observes that the sexual vulnerability of Black women greatly impacts cultural attitudes and strategies of public presentation, i.e., dress and comportment. In a struggle for their dignity and autonomy, Black women deployed a culture of dissemblance, in which "black women as a rule, developed and adhered to a cult of secrecy, a culture of dissemblance, to protect the sanctity of inner aspects of their lives" (p. 915).

43 Migos, Nicki Minaj, and Cardi B, "Motorsport," track 17 on *Culture II*, Quality Control, Motown and Capitol Records, 2018.

44 Missy Elliott, "I'm Better," recorded 2017, Goldmind and Atlantic Records.

notions of sex appeal and declares herself a sexually desirable and desiring subject. Taking pleasure in her ebony skin and larger frame, which she moves with confidence and command, Missy defies Western aesthetical values and uses sexually charged lyrics and choreography to celebrate her Black sexual body and her authority over it. Megan Thee Stallion solidifies expression of sexual pleasure as a foundational element of the female rapper. Employing the same raucus linguistic device as Minaj and Elliott, the femcee raps about her sexual prowess with a verve and confidence that dominant notions of femininity consider taboo.

Raunchy sexual language is not limited to rap. Though more discreetly coded in euphemism and double-entendre, crossover artist Rihanna croons about sauce on lips that do not belong to her mouth to assert her own sexual agency. Whether in spite of these cultural, racial, and gendered transgressions or because of them, these artists have risen to the heights of mainstream success in the music industry. Their lyrical sexual bravado depicts them as women who unapologetically enjoy sexual pleasure while simultaneously improving their status as desirable and knowledgeable sexual partners. Referred to as sexual entrepreneurship, the seeming hypervisibility of some Provocatrixters' sexuality not only affords them a freedom often resigned to men, it also bolsters their sexual capital in a system that privileges sexual desirability, generating more money and exposure, and therefore more power.[45]

For women who have been historically dispossessed of authority over their relational bodies, personhoods, and faculties, sex can become a mode of self-possession and outlet for expressions of self-love and empowerment.

45 Much of the raunchy talk deployed by provocateurs is deployed as spectacle—theatrical sexuality used to draw attention. Off stage, provocateurs continue in the tradition of dissemblance, maintaining privacy about their sexualities and personal relationships. Beyoncé, who has maintained a monogamous relationship with rapper Jay Z for more than ten years, kept the world guessing about the status of their relationship well into the first year of their marriage. Nicki Minaj also draws a line of distinction between her celebrity persona and personal life. Most recently she was romantically linked to rapper Nas. In a 2017 interview on the talk show *Ellen*, Minaj remained tight-lipped about the extent of the couple's sexual activity, claiming the two were friends who enjoyed sleepovers, but were refraining from sexual relations. Missy Elliott has also been private about her sexuality, which was the subject of much conjecture in the press. When questioned about rumors that she was same-gender loving, Missy offered no clarity, but used the opportunity to critique sexual gender politics, commenting on society's confusion when they see an independent, powerful woman. For more, see Theresa Renee White, "Missy 'Misdemeanor' Elliott and Nicki Minaj Fashionistin' Black Female Sexuality in Hip-Hop Culture—Girl Power or Overpowered?," *Journal of Black Studies* 44, no. 6 (2013): 607–26.

And those expressions can, in turn, empower others. In influential musician Lizzo's 2021 Ted Talk, she recalls the impact Beyoncé's twerking in her 2003 "Crazy in Love" video had on Lizzo's beliefs about her body and its power. "I wanted to be just like her," she said, "to be myself, to be seen as bootylicious, to be bootylicious and still be classy." But hegemony does not register Black women, especially larger Black women, as sexually desirable. When they express themselves sexually, it is often decried as excessively crude.[46] Lizzo's words express the longing Black women feel to live beyond the significations of the hegemonic imagination and to be free to fully engage the sexual power of their bodies without being villainized. For Lizzo, Beyoncé's twerk offered more than an image. It offered an experience of the sensual Black body being celebrated in and for its seductiveness, inspiring Lizzo to indulge in the practice as well. And through that experience, she argues, she found her magic.[47]

Lizzo's is a story of triumph. However, to resist facile celebrations that distance strategies of reclamation from the pain and abuse of dispossession, we must heed Katie Cannon's admonishment to take into account "the circumstances, the paradoxes, and the dilemmas that constrict Blacks to the lowest ranges of self-determination."[48] Accordingly, we cannot dismiss the ways the meanings of sex and desire for Black women have been hidden and distorted in the silences that guard legacies of rape, child molestation, exploitation, dehumanization, and despair. We cannot ignore the ways even Black desire has been shaped by the debasing gaze of anti-Blackness and misogyny. We cannot look away from the political status, economic power, and psychic peace these realities rob from Black human beings such that their choices are always circumscribed by the dominion of white and male desire.

For instance, Harriet Jacobs's *Incidents in the Life of a Slave Girl* describes the unorthodox strategies she found necessary to evade the unwanted sexual

---

46 Responses to Lizzo's butt-bearing leggings included one detractor offering, "These are the same women who demand to be respected and treated with dignity. . . . Yet they act like animals. If any man were to expose himself in public the way that Lizzo has, he would be called a sexual predator. But she's a brave, confident hero for strutting around nearly naked." For more, see Amanda Harding, "'Not Attractive or Healthy: Twitter Rips Lizzo for Baring Her Entire Butt in Promo for Yitty Shapewear," DailyWire, April 12, 2022, https://www.dailywire.com/news/lizzo-bares-her-entire-butt-in-revealing-new-instagram-promo-for-yitty-shapewear.

47 Lizzo, "The Black History of Twerking and How It Taught Me Self-Love," video, TED Conferences, September 2021, https://www.ted.com/talks/lizzo_the_black_history_of_twerking_and_how_it_taught_me_self_love?language=en.

48 Cannon, *Black Womanist Ethics*, 3.

advances of Dr. Flint, the lecherous white man who owned her. Throughout her narrative of events, Jacobs repeatedly begs the reader to understand the peril of inspiring the libidinous desires of someone with complete dominion over her body and her life. She writes,

> Pity me and pardon me, O virtuous reader! You never knew what it is to be a slave; to be entirely unprotected by law or custom; to have the laws reduce you to the condition of chattel, entirely subject to the will of another. You never exhausted your ingenuity in avoiding the snares, and eluding the power of a hated tyrant; you never shuddered at the sound of his footsteps, and trembled within hearing of his voice. I know I did wrong. No one can feel it more sensibly than I do. The painful and humiliating memory will haunt me to my dying day. Still in looking back calmly, on the events of my life, I feel that the slave woman ought not be judged by the same standard as others.[49]

The tyranny of her master's desires demanded Jacobs submit her body—herself—to a white man, who was not her husband. Incompatible with Christian understandings of virtue and purity and the prevailing Victorian rubric of femininity within American culture, Jacobs's choices illustrate the ways Black women's bodily dispossession obscures the dynamics of Black sexuality. Thus, Black women's sexual lives often fail to fit neatly into normative ethical values of purity, consent, innocence, and pleasure, making the entire concept of sexual agency, as it pertains to Black women, a contestable category. Rather than emanating from the freedom philosophers like Aristotle and Kant lionized, moral agency for Jacobs consists of choices made in unfreedom, composed of a lack of body right, and pallid agency, which according to Aristotle is limited by the virtue of one's master.[50]

Enslaved Black women's sexual virtue was overdetermined by the sexual volition of their masters and the ever-present sexual precarity their masters created or allowed. Their bodies did not belong to them, but to those who owned them, underscoring again the need for strategies for Black women to repossess their bodies and reclaim their ability to self-authorize. Historian William Dusinberre, through the testimonies of those formerly in bondage in the state of Virginia,

---

49 Harriet A. Jacobs, *Incidents in the Life of a Slave Girl: Written By Herself*, ed. Jean Fagan Yellin (Boston: Thayer & Eldridge, 1861; repr., Cambridge, MA: Harvard University Press, 1987), 55–56.

50 In *Nicomachean Ethics*, Aristotle argues that the moral agent is circumscribed by his ability to reason, judge, and *choose, free of coercion*. It is the freedom of the will that determines moral choice in human agents. While reason guides the process of deliberation, it is freedom that enables ownership of an action by an agent.

recounts that it was common practice for white men to exploit Black women sexually.[51] In the aftermath of these sexual assaults, Black women had little recourse to protect themselves or exact justice. For in the eyes of America's legal system, Black women possessed uncontrollable, insatiable sexual appetites and could therefore not be raped. These controlling images or narratives that sought to justify sexual violence against Black women shaped not only how they were perceived, but how they performed sexuality. Forcing Black women into hiding and suppressing their sexualities, for the sake of respectability, they created what theologian Kelly Brown Douglas describes as a discourse of silence, a general ethic of silence about and regarding Black women's sexual lives.[52]

Narratives about Black women's sexualities, constructed by the dominant culture, continue to inform Black women's sexual expression and agency more broadly to this day. Despite the emancipation of Black women after the Civil War, their sexual vulnerability remained a major threat in their lives, such that in addition to fighting for the dignity of the Black woman's image, Black clubwomen in the early twentieth century also took action to preserve the dignity of their bodies. During this time, Black women often existed as prey in the homes of white men, where they worked as domestics. Hoping to distance would-be domestics from danger, clubwomen worked hard to provide opportunities for poor and working-class women to gain skills that would move them out of the homes of white people and into office work. Detailing her own near sexual assault by the white man she worked for as a maid, revered civil rights activist Rosa Parks penned a letter expressing an unmovable determination not to be sexually exploited.[53] Despite the ways refusal might lead to financial loss, or worse—the brutal enforcement of "Mr. Charlie's" will—Parks literally fought the man off, writing, "I was willing to die. But give my consent, never. Never, never."[54] Parks's words convey an unexpected yet deeply grounded sense of sexual agency for the times and the keen awareness that the assertion of her agency—her refusal—could mean her life. Such was the reality for many Black women, who were dependent on domestic work for their economic livelihood. To avoid such work and therefore danger, the

---

51 William Dusinberre, *Strategies for Survival, Recollections of Bondage in Antebellum Virginia* (Charlottesville: University of Virginia Press, 2009), 32–33.

52 Douglas, *Sexuality and the Black Church*, 67.

53 Rosa Parks, Rosa Parks Papers: Writings, Notes, and Statements, 1956-1998; Drafts of early writings; Autobiographical, circa 1956, undated, Library of Congress, Washington, DC, https://www.loc.gov/item/mss859430227.

54 Rosa Parks, image 18 of Rosa Parks Papers.

performance of a bawdy sexuality for entertainment became blues women's path to freedom from both domestic work and domesticity.

Contemporary sexual politics continue to demand transgression in Black women's assertion of power and self-possession. More than 150 years after slavery, Black women's bodies continue to be the locus upon which male power is demonstrated. Though they have reached record-breaking heights in education, buying power, and position, Black women continue to be the primary outlet for the displaced lust for power, anger, and sexual aggression of intimate partners who believe themselves entitled to dominate and exploit their bodies.[55] For example, in 2022, Megan The Stallion was shot in the feet by fellow rapper Tory Lanez for injuring his pride in an argument over who had the more successful career. After she was shot, numerous media outlets and the music industry further victimized the femcee by calling her a liar for reporting the incident and for her denial of having had sexual relations with Lanez. In defense of Lanez, popular hip-hop platforms like *The Joe Budden Podcast*, DJ Akademiks, and Math Hoffa's *My Expert Opinion* presented Megan as violent, promiscuous, an alcoholic, and unethical in business, turning the responsibility for the incident on the victim, rather than the perpetrator.

Still, male domination in the form of violence is just one manner in which Black women's bodies are transgressed. Governmental and institutional powers that parasitically benefit from their labor, intellectual capital, and the fruits of their wombs withhold basic bodily freedoms and justice from Black women. From the right to manage their own reproductive capacities, to safe working conditions in factory labor, medical justice, and even the right to adorn their hair as they see fit, Black women's dignity, which freedom fighter Ella Baker believed was synonymous with the right to control one's own body, is regularly denied Black women.[56] Within a Black church context,

---

55 For more, see Brittney Nanton, "The Treatment of Megan Thee Stallion Further Exposes Society's Hatred of Black Women," Girls United, April 27, 2022, https://girlsunited.essence.com/article/megan-thee-stallion-shot-allegations/; and Evan Malbrough, "Op-Ed: Megan Thee Stallion and Other Black Women Deserve Better," BET, Dec. 19, 2022, https://www.bet.com/article/5exuc3/op-ed-megan-thee-stallion-other-black-women-deserve-better.

56 For more information on the mistreatment of Black women in the United States on a institutional and personal level, see "#SayHerName," African American Policy Forum, https://www.aapf.org/sayhername; Patricia Hill Collins, *Black Feminist Thought: Knowledge, Consciousness, and the Politics of Empowerment* (New York: Routledge, 2000); Stephanie R. Bush-Baskette, *Misguided Justice: The War on Drugs and the Incarceration of Black Women* (Bloomington, IN: iUniverse, 2010); Shatema Threadcraft, *Intimate Justice: The Black Female and the Body Politic* (New York: Oxford University Press, 2016); and

Black women suffer, existing as bodies with no political power, and remain scapegoats of the community's ills and depositories of blame. Womanist ethicists Marcia Riggs and Chanequa Walker-Barnes have underscored the political and institutional disenfranchisement Black women experience in the Black church and the Black community and the manner in which both continue to exploit Black women's bodily labor, while requests for sustained and intentional advocacy from the same institutions fall on deaf ears.[57]

CORPOREAL INCANTATIONS

Provocatrixters' music, lyrics, and dance represent a pathway of escape from the limits of sexual-gender oppression for everyday Black women. Their participation in the sexually charged performances of these cultural icons project ritual significance or religious meaning in the world, orienting those who watch to the new status and power of Black women. In the ritual sense, these bodily performances generate the image of a powerful Black woman, facilitating a transformation of identities and the empowerment of Black women through the exercising of their sexual selves.[58] Both the religious fascination with celebrity and the sexual power Provocatrixters invoke contribute to a ritual practice of freedom. As Black women emulate the self-possession and autonomy Provocatrixters proffer by singing their lyrics, imitating their dances, and adopting their sexual gender politics, they create themselves anew. Commenting on the role of hip-hop in shaping the worldviews of Black youth, Africana studies scholar Imani Perry describes hip-hop as "a space of transgression, where new identities and radicalized Black subjectivities emerge."[59] Consequently Black people, especially Black girls, flock to hip-hop for its liberative possibilities and consider its practices and aesthetics empowering. Patricia Hill Collins expounds upon the influence of Black popular culture:

> In modern America where community institutions of all sorts have eroded, popular culture has increased in importance as a source of information and

---

Enobong Hannah Branch, *Opportunity Denied: Limiting Black Women to Devalued Work* (Piscataway, NJ: Rutgers University Press, 2011).

57 For more, see Riggs, *Plenty Good Room*; and Walker-Barnes, *Too Heavy a Yoke.*

58 Smith, *Conjuring Culture*, 57–58.

59 Imani Perry, *Prophets of the Hood: Politics and Poetics in Hip-Hop* (Durham, NC: Duke University Press, 2004), 122.

ideas. African-American youth in particular, can no longer depend on a deeply textured web of families, churches, fraternal organizations . . . and other community organizations to help them negotiate the challenges of social inequality. Mass media fills this void, especially movies, television and music that market Black popular culture aimed at African American Consumers.[60]

Provocatrixters' incantatory strategy of conjuring a more powerful identity differs little from of clubwomen's strategies of conjuring a more respectable Black womanhood in the early 1900s. Both deploy a sense of identity and esteem generated from their own experiences and values that enable postures of authority in their relations with a more politically powerful other.[61] While clubwomen's defiant assertion of their value leveraged American Christian sexual social mores to assert worth through moral superiority, Provocatrixters contest the validity of these ideologies through the performative manipulation of their sexualities as a means of asserting bodily autonomy and therefore freedom.

Shifting from the politics of respectability to a politics of authority, Provocatrixters' sexual spectacle is intended to be combative. It provokes on purpose. Their in-your-face antics not only embrace the taboo behaviors white Christian Americans so fear, but mock them through sexualized spectacles in celebration of themselves.[62] Rather than conceal their sexuality, as was the way of the clubwoman, Provocatrixters, like their blues women forebears, present the transgressive practice of desire and sexual expression as a resource that can be used to produce agential power in the lives of Black women. Free of the psychic handicap of double consciousness, this twenty-first-century embodied radical subjectivity conjures a world in the subaltern where Black women themselves define the parameters and set the rules of engagement.

WHEN THE POISON IS THE CURE

To be sure, Provocatrixters trade in stereotypically sexist notions of sexually assertive women. Rather than fight against the inevitability of the commodification of culture and identity, however, Provocatrixters exploit its

---

60 Patricia Hill Collins, *Black Sexual Politics: African Americans, Gender, and the New Racism* (New York: Routledge, 2001), 121–22.

61 Kimberly Foster, "Wrestling with Respectability in the Age of #BlackLivesMatter," *For Harriet*, October 13, 2015, http://www.forharriet.com/2015/10/wrestling-with-respectability-in-age-of.html#axzz4f0ufsrWp.

62 Elliott, "I'm Better"; Lizzo, "The Black History of Twerking."

consumption by the dominant culture. Despite the selfish gains of white corporations from their craft, for Provocatrixters, the market provides a vehicle into the hearts, minds, and wallets of millions who devour Black culture as a right.[63] Instead of deconstructing or considering the impact of the structures of the social imagination that make stereotypes possible, Provocatrixters pragmatically operate as tricksters within them. These tricks create a pathway to survival and in some cases flourishing.

Audre Lorde writes, "In order to survive, those of us for whom oppression is as American as apple pie have always had to be watchers. This 'watching' generates a dual consciousness in African-American women, one in which Black women become familiar with the language and manners of the oppressor, even sometimes adopting them for some illusion of protection."[64] Thee Smith's account of homeopathic magic is helpful in understanding the duality of Provocatrixters. He explains that homeopathic magic relies on relationships of similarity that are used to embody or direct the magic of conjure "for good or ill in order to benefit or harm."[65] In this case, "the practitioner typically uses a skillfully prepared or modified dosage of a disease in order to cure the disease."[66] For the Provocatrixter, the disease of concern is the imposition of hegemony's truncated identities (the Mammy, the Sapphire, the Jezebel) upon Black women. In keeping with Smith's logic, I argue the remedy demands a modified dose of the same. Using a little of the poison of racist patriarchy's significations to liberate them from the cages these significations create, Provocatrixters conjure the phantasms of the white moral imagination's nightmares. Challenging the fantastic hegemonic imagination as a monolith by operating within it, the conjure of Provocatrixters represents their construction of a homeopathic counterhegemony—their attempt to interrupt hegemony with their own voices, "to tell the story a different way," and as a result, transform their realities.[67]

Counterhegemony signifies deliberate artificial inventions used to negotiate a meaningful existence in contemporary society.[68] Inspired by womanist ethicist Emilie Townes's use of the term coined by Antonio Gramsci, my use of counterhegemony represents microhistories, or narratives created and

63 Townes, *Womanist Ethics*, 3, 6.
64 Lorde, "Uses of the Erotic," 114.
65 Smith, *Conjuring Culture*, 27–28, 169.
66 Smith, *Conjuring Culture*, 168.
67 Smith, *Conjuring Culture*, 5, 7.
68 Townes, *Womanist Ethics*, 14.

recreated by dispossessed communities in response to deleterious political and social circumstances that stifle them.[69] These narratives are often silenced. In defiance of the silencing of the moral philosophies of the oppressed, and leaning into their potential to impact the social imagination, Provocatrixters mobilize Black sexuality as a spiritual force of seductive coercion, for the aggressive inclusion of Black women as more than dominated objects in the moral and social imagination.[70] Townes contends that images, or what I am calling phantasms, are produced by the interplay of imagination and history acting as truth.[71] The phantasms of Provocatrixters, however, are the interplay of imagination and art conjuring a new reality as truth.

The new phantasms conjured by Provocatrixters are images of the reviled, remixed in the tradition of hip-hop, to create a version of unapologetic Black female power of their own construction. Images of this power can be found in Black women's bodywork, otherwise understood as body stylization, body language, and sexual and gender performances (and the cultural expression that the body generates). Generated from the real bodies of Black women, these images, I contend, are products of the haptic, yet they operate in the realm of the imagination. Rather than the persona of one, they represent the sum of the strategies of many, facilitating alternative experiences of Black flesh that seduce or enchant those who experience them to such a degree that they want to celebrate, participate in, and know more fully the sexually autonomous, willful, self-possessed, self-determined, Black female agent embodied by the Provocatrixter. As such, the power she conjures is also a pathway to a kind of radical subjectivity or self-definition for Black women who choose to live into this persona. Accordingly, both the Provocatrixters and the women who deploy these corporeal incantations represent a conjurational performance that has been historically transformative and therapeutic. As homeopathic images of counterhegemony, they open up the space to interrogate accepted structures of domination—the very work of erotic defiance. And yet, those practices of liberation can easily become performances. Counterhegenomies do not always prevail.

For example, in recent years it has been revealed that a Provocatrixter like Lil' Kim, one of the first female rappers to deploy sexual transgression to assert her autonomy, was simply reciting lyrics that The Notorious

---

69 Townes, *Womanist Ethics*, 17.
70 Townes, *Womanist Ethics*, 17.
71 Townes, *Womanist Ethics*, 12–14.

B.I.G. wrote for her, performing, in essence, what a Black man imagined the power of Black female sexuality to be. Even those femcees who actually write their own rhymes continue to present power in the key of patriarchal violence through lyrics that showcase the sexual domination and disparagement of women. Even Lizzo, who has been successful in moving beyond the traditional tropes of patriarchal demonstrations of power, maintains a standard of relevance deeply situated in tropes of Black women's sexuality as capital, declaring her butt—not her flute, imagination, or talent—as her best asset.[72]

Townes is instructive here. She points out that the power of influence, manifested through force or persuasion, facilitates the interpretation and perception of the world in a particular way, typically favoring the maintenance of power by a particular dominating group.[73] She writes, "We often operate out of structurally determined limits that do, at points, offer some creativity and autonomy—but these are always controlled and managed by hegemonic forces of an exploitative industry."[74] Indeed, the self-possessed, autonomous agent that raps, sings, and dances into our imaginations is herself haunted by the demand that she look and perform a certain way. Lizzo has had the blessing of being a transgressive outlier, but most images made available to the masses follow what Nicki Minaj calls the "female rapper starter kit," which includes "pink wig, thick ass, give 'em whip lash."[75] For those who don't have the bodies the male gaze requires, dangerous and sometimes life-threatening plastic surgery, like Brazilian butt lifts, breast augmentation, and liposuction have become initiation rituals as well as practices in the maintenance of power.[76]

---

72 Lizzo, "The Black History of Twerking."

73 Townes, *Womanist Ethics*, 20.

74 Townes, *Womanist Ethics*, 18–19.

75 "A Conversation with Nicki Minaj & Joe Budden," YouTube, Joe Budden TV, March 9, 2022, https://www.youtube.com/watch?v=LSmMQEsBzmE.

76 "From 2005 to 2013, the American Society of Aesthetic Plastic Surgery found that Black patients increased by 56 percent. In 2016, 8 percent of all plastic surgery procedures were for Black patients, doubling the percentage from 1997. Women who cannot afford professional treatments have resorted to home remedies that include deadly and illegal injections with a toxic substance to accomplish their desired look. These home remedies sometimes result in death, and those who do survive are left with debilitating scars and lingering health issues." For more, see Dominque R. Wilson, "Sexual Exploitation of Black Women from the Years 1619–2020," *Journal of Race, Gender, and Ethnicity* 10 (Spring 2021): 128.

WHERE IS THE LOVE? SEXUAL
CONJURE TO WHAT END?

While combative and entrepreneurial sexuality imaged by the Provocatrixter continues in the curative tradition of conjure, those embracing sexual forms of conjure must contend with the fact that without the power and security of selfhood and social protection, hegemonic traditions and dynamics of power will reassert themselves. Though many would paint Harriet Jacobs's sexual choices as entrepreneurial seduction, with no protection from sexual assault, Jacobs's so-called agency equates to decisions made in unfreedom, and at best a salvaging of her dignity from the unchecked desires her body drew. Rather than erotic seduction, the appropriate categorization of these kinds of coercive scenarios is the pornographic—the use of Black women's bodies with no regard for their humanity. For the desire these bodies draw is saturated with the legacy of Black women's being used as sexual chattel. Within this libidinal calculus, sexual domination was another expression of white men's right as God's chosen for dominion over the earth. It is only within the context of the authority of the desire of racist patriarchy that Black women's sexual agency can appropriately be calculated. Thus, the functions of traditional categories of love, consent, pleasure, and desire continue to be difficult to determine. Given that these acts supersede the logic of traditional ethical rubrics, how can we account for the sexually transgressive power of the Provocatrixters when all too often these performances of sexuality are mired in the power and desire of racist patriarchy? If conjure is to be erotic defiance and not commodified performance, we must ask, Where is love? Where is God?

Africana scholar Kameelah Martin contends that the cultural idiom of conjure defies the estrangement of spirit and sexuality. In fact, like many Black feminists and womanists, she posits that Black women's sexuality is a primary manifestation of the divine. Highlighting the ways Black women's literature describes the body as vessel in the phenomenon of spiritual possession, how spirits fit "neatly into sinews, bones and blood," and the experience of spiritual occupation as a "a pleasurable act of submission" in which the conjuror "gives her body over to the whims of a spirit, rejoicing over her connection to the spirit world,"[77] she describes sexuality as more than just pleasure-seeking

---

77 Kameelah Martin, *Conjuring Moments in African American Literature: Women, Spirit Work, and Other Such Hoodoo* (New York: Palgrave Macmillan, 2012), 121.

impulses, but a conduit of spiritual knowledge and power. But if in fact Black female sexuality is a manifestation of the divine and therefore God, then like the erotic, its fruit should be love.

In search of these fruits, I turn to Black women's interiority and what participation in these performances do in and for their flesh. Through their compelling performances-turned-rituals of corporeal incantation, Provoca-trixters' postures of sexual resistance seduce Black women's imaginations into a love of their body selves. Showering Black women in images that posit Black female bodies as desiring and desirable, they offer their audiences experiences of celebration of and practice in invoking their sexual dynamism, forging self-love based on new understandings of the power of their bodies and sexualities. These bodies command authority. They move and give expression to a force that unites flesh and Spirit through sexuality, reconnecting Black women to the sacred voice within. Self-love can also be understood as a preference for this voice and the truth it speaks, which typically sounds like defiance of the status quo. Katie Cannon argues, "The Black woman's [and I would argue all subjects' othered by white supremacy] very life depends upon . . . their ability to resist the demand to capitulate to the status quo."[78] The status quo in this case is acceptance of the ideology of Black inferiority and the desecration of Black sexuality. It is the preference and esteem for everything white. Defiance is rooted in a profound sense of self-love, which animates the rejection of ideas that diminish a sense of self-worth and allows one to embrace one's self as "divinely and humanly loveable."[79] Cannon argues defiance is "a refusal to be inwardly brutalized."[80] This refusal enables the kind of persistence that "allows Black women to continue taking risks against limits that deny their beingness."[81] Using the words of Zora Neale Hurston, Cannon lauds the practice of defiance as "the determination to please one's self when tradition fails to satisfy."[82] The ability to survive, be free, and actualize one's potential in the world requires the defiance of powers of oppression through the affirmation of one's own identity as good and worthy.

---

78 Cannon, *Black Womanist Ethics*, 126.

79 Cheryl Gilkes Townsend, "A Conscious Connection to All That Is: *The Color Purple* as Subversive and Critical Ethnography," in *Embracing the Spirit: Womanist Perspectives on Hope, Salvation and Transformation*, ed. Emilie Townes (Maryknoll, NY: Orbis Books, 1997), 275–96, via Floyd-Thomas, *Deeper Shades of Purple*, 10.

80 Cannon, *Black Womanist Ethics*, 127.

81 Cannon, *Black Womanist Ethics*, 133–34.

82 Cannon, *Black Womanist Ethics*, 135.

Consequently, erotic defiance as a subversive ethical discipline exposes the fallacy of Western assessments of Black identity and morality through Black women's activity in the world and legitimizes Black women's experiences as vital resources for ethical reflection. It also constructs new possibilities that result from these resources and revelations.[83] This struggle against self-alienating values toward a deeper sense of community and wholeness is predicated upon maintaining a posture of determination, perseverance, and self-love. [84] Whether twerking, undulating, or other erotic forms of dance, Black women practice the pleasure and power of sexuality and the spiritual connection to one's flesh. As Margaret Walker Alexander avers, sexuality includes our spiritual selves. It is by the aid of the erotic, experienced in practices of self-celebration and the connection between spirit and flesh it affords, that the oppressed, specifically Black men and women, bear witness to the fallacy of racist patriarchal formulations of their identity.

The expression of sexuality through dance becomes an opportunity, then, to practice bodily self-possession, an integral feature of freedom for individuals dispossessed of their bodies. As theological essayist Candice Benbow writes in her review of Beyoncé's controversial, boundary-breaking song, "Church Girls," "Something supernatural happens when we tap into the power of loving ourselves." Like Lizzo, Benbow believes sexual dance is holy and can be a catalyst for self-love.[85] I would not argue with her. Surely a healthy understanding of one's sexuality as one's own, and of pleasure as a right, constitutive of human freedom, are crucial aspects of Black women's reclamation of their bodies. However, I am not convinced that the experience of sexual power and pleasure and the exercising of desire in and of themselves make Black women free or arbiters of the erotic.

Once these practices move beyond the veil of intimacy and are performed for mass consumption, they are often plundered for their power and robbed of their sacrality by the same forces that attempt to deny the Black female subject social, political, and economic autonomy. Their choreography of sexual authority and the posture of a desiring subject is performed, but the spirit is preempted. Practice turned performance is obscured by pornotroping, a gaze

---

83 Marcia Riggs, *Awake, Arise & Act: A Womanist Call for Black Liberation* (Cleveland: Pilgrim, 1994), 2.

84 Cannon, *Black Womanist Ethics*, 132.

85 Candice Marie Benbow, "Beyoncé Invites Church Girls to Celebrate Their Freedom," Religious News Service, July 30, 2022, https://religionnews.com/2022/07/30/renaissance-beyonce-invites-church-girls-to-celebrate-their-freedom/.

that perverts with its demands for satisfaction.[86] Practice turned performance transforms erotic defiance into combative sexuality. It deforms the beauty and creative power of sex into a weapon to be used for mocking disapproving onlookers, or for climbing in status through the exploitation of sexual partners and even one's own body. In such scenarios, sex becomes spectacle, a means to an end. However, the goal of the erotic is transformation, not transaction.

Despite their liberative intentions, these sexual performances take on the American capitalistic ethos of prioritizing economic gain, pleasure, and profit. Rather than transcending or transforming traditional constructions of the erotic, they often mimic the rhetoric of erotophobia. They fetishize Black sexuality, while presenting a counterfeit account of its power, truncating Black corporeality's erotic attributes to sexual arousal alone. In this schema, Black women's bodies are good, but only for the desires they elicit, the pursuit of individual pleasure, money-making, and amassing power. These formulas of power, however, do not exceed or challenge the scripts of domination through desire.

VEILING LIKE VASHTI

The liberation erotic defiance affords is found in the ways practices of self-celebration and self-possession reconnect Black women to the sacred power of their bodies and sexualities. Accordingly, to preserve the power of what these practices produce within Black women, ordinary Black women practicing the sexual chords of erotic defiance might be better served by leaving sexual spectacle to the Provocatrixters, whose artistry, wealth, and fame in some ways shield them from the violence visited upon defiant women, and instead utilizing an ethic of veiling. Though the metaphor of the veil conjures the historic silencing of Black women's sexuality, an ethic of veiling is intended to promote wisdom, protection, and the right of refusal that amplifies the sacrality of Black women's sexuality, their sexual sovereignty, and the reality of Black women's moral situation. Taking as its reference points the veil of Moses

---

86 Pornotroping is a way of seeing with both the eyes and the psyche that is simultaneously othering. For more, see Tamura Lomax, *Jezebel Unhinged: Losing the Black Female Body in Religion and Culture* (Durham, NC: Duke University Press, 2018); and Hortense Spillers, *Black, White, and in Color: Essays on American Literature and Culture* (Chicago: University of Chicago Press, 2003).

or the traditional white cloth placed in front of the communion elements in Black Baptist churches, an ethic of veiling highlights the awesomeness and terribleness of the power of human sexuality.[87] Calling attention to the ways human sexuality images God's very nature, it reverences its remarkable power, tempering it with an acknowledgement that when handled without care, it can become a terrible problem for those in its wake.[88] While this generation is known for its unwillingness to shrink in the face of white opposition and operates out of a politics of authority, the reality is Black women rarely go toe-to-toe with empire and win. As the chapter has demonstrated, power for the oppressed has most often been a Trixter's game, a covert seduction that inoculates one's adversary before they even realize they are engaged in warfare. As the fictional story of the beating and imprisonment of Sophia in Alice Walker's *The Color Purple* or the celebration of Sha'Carri Richardson's loss and disqualification from the 2020 Tokyo Olympics demonstrates, Black women who are self-possessed (unabashedly owning their worth, their talent, and their power) are offensive to the world, especially the Black community.[89] As the fictional crowd that gathered to beat Sophia and the very real angry Twitter mob, comprised of both Black and white users, attest, the world seeks not only to subdue Black women who make displays of their power, but to harass, ridicule, and even violently beat them into submission or slander their names to remind them that according the dominant worldview they have no right to think highly of themselves.

Accordingly, the veil provides protection. The veil, in the case of Moses, who spoke intimately with God, face-to-face, served to mediate access, such that he could revel in the awesomeness and terribleness of God's glory without harming himself or his Israelite followers since the beauty and terrible glory of God shone on his face even after he had come down from worshipping on

---

87 Exodus 34:33–35.

88 Here I liken the power of sexuality to the power of God's glory in Deuteronomy. For more on the power and danger of the glory of God, see Walter Brueggemann, *Ichabod Toward Home: The Journey of God's Glory* (Eugene, OR: Wipf and Stock, 2002).

89 Walker, *The Color Purple*, 85–87. For more on Sha'Carri Richardson, see Kunal Dey, "Sha'Carri Richardson trolled for finishing last at Prefontaine Classic," MEAWW.COM, August 22, 2021, https://meaww.com/prefontaine-classic-shacarri-richardson-finishing-last-marijuana-suspension; and Jacob Gijy, "'Gotta Be More Professional'-Sha'Carri Richardson Faces Twitter Heat for Her Behaviour With Media Post Upsetting Loss," Essentially Sports, June 24, 2022, https://www.essentiallysports.com/us-sports-news-track-and-field-news-gotta-be-more-professional-shacarri-richardson-faces-twitter-heat-for-her-behaviour-with-media-post-upsetting-loss/.

Mount Horeb. However, it is important to emphasize that it was not the glory that shone on Moses's face that was the problem, but the lack of the capacity of the people's gaze. The Israelites were incapable of beholding the glory of God. Their sin obscured that which was beautiful, life-giving, and transformative into something potentially death dealing. Similarly, the gaze of the audience matters in the display of the glory of Black women's sexuality. This includes the disapproving gaze, shaped by the Western moral imagination and its disciplining powers that have historically disciplined Black women for stepping out of line. Perhaps more importantly, an ethic of veiling considers young people and sexual assault survivors, many of whom are Black and continue to find themselves in sexually compromising scenarios against their will. Though slavery has ended, tawdry propositions continue to be whispered in the ears of young girls and even boys, as assailants with more power impose their sexualities upon them. Here I am thinking of sexual spectacles like the exposure of intimate parts of our bodies, in the name of freedom, like the cheeks of our behinds in public spaces for the consumption of all. In light of how complicated Black women's own relationship with sexual consent has been, it seems only just that we consider the importance of consent before imposing our sexualities onto others. In this way, an ethic of veiling functions reciprocally, protecting Black women from the violence of a desecrating and disciplining gaze and protecting those with a history of sexual abuse from the imposition of another's sexuality.

In the case of Moses, veiling enacts protection; however, an ethic of veiling is also inspired by Queen Vashti, the first wife of King Ahasuerus, and her refusal to display her sexual glory to her husband's friends for sport.[90] As such, an ethic of veiling also signifies Black women's refusal to allow others to control their sexualities. It asserts that they themselves are the final authority on who will have access to their charms and who will not. Consequently, the ethic does not serve to suppress or disconnect Black women from the power of the erotic, but to recognize it as holy, set apart, as discriminating regarding who has the honor to participate. Moreover, emphasis on the holy and sacred power of the erotic is instrumental to a liberative ethic of erotic power for

---

90 The exiling of Vashti is often understood as punishment for her unwillingness to "dance" before the king and his friends. This is understood by scholars as a request for something akin to a striptease. For more, see Deborah F. Sawyer, "Queen Vashti's 'No' and What It Can Tell Us about Gender Tools In Biblical Narrative," in *The Bible and Feminism: Remapping the Field*, ed. Yvonne Sherwood (New York: Oxford University Press, 2017) 1–13.

marginalized communities—especially Black and female communities that struggle with the denigration of their bodies and their agency on a daily basis. As the prevalence of combative and opportunistic sexuality demonstrates, Black women and girls are often given two approaches toward their sexual power: stifle it, as religious communities and institutions have taught them to do, or wield it as a weapon, seeing it as one of the few tools they have with which to navigate through life. Framing the erotic as sacred in all its awesome and terrible glory resists disconnecting Black women's bodies from the legacies of pain they have endured. It does not dismiss the terribleness that can arise in the abuse of sexuality as seen in Black women's and girls' molestation, sexual exploitation, and commodification, and its mismanagement as seen in combative sexuality.[91] As Black women reclaim our bodies and celebrate, we must remember that Black women continue to be the most vulnerable to sex trafficking in the United States, due to the discursive designations cultivated by misogynoir, making up about 40 percent of all victims of sex trafficking. The market also continues to exploit Black women for profit, even in their celebrations of self-love. For example Yolanda Norton, creator of the Beyoncé Mass, a sacred celebration of Black women inspired by the music of Beyoncé, suggests that while Lizzo's brand of self-love is most certainly a win for Black women, it too is extracted and commodified as a powerful marketing strategy for women's consumption of Yitty athletic wear, tickets to concerts, and

---

91 For more, see National Black Women's Justice Institute, "Sex Trafficking of Black Women & Girls Fact Sheet," January 2022; and Ann Schmidt, "What Is Lizzo's Net Worth?," FoxBusiness, February 7, 2020, https://www.foxbusiness.com/money/what-is-lizzos-net-worth. The impact of Black women being used for their bodies by sexual partners is a prevailing theme in hip-hop as male rappers and those who emulate them wax on about using Black women for sex and disposing of them later. Additionally, the CDC reports that Black women in the United States experience STIs at an alarming proportion, including HIV: "In 2012, compared with white women, African American women were more likely to be diagnosed with primary or secondary syphilis, gonorrhea, or chlamydia (16.3, 13.8, and 6.2 times, respectively). African American women were also two to three times as likely as white women to have pelvic inflammatory disease. If left undiagnosed or untreated, these conditions can lead to pregnancy complications and infertility. In addition, the CDC reported that African American women had an HIV incidence rate that was 20.1 times greater than that of white women in 2010. African American women are also more likely to have delayed HIV treatment compared with women of other races." Cynthia Prather et al., "Racism, African American Women, and Their Sexual and Reproductive Health: A Review of Historical and Contemporary Evidence and Implications for Health Equity," *Health Equity* 2, no. 1 (2018): 249–59, here 252–53, doi:10.1089/heq.2017.0045.

various products that line the pockets of corporate entities.[92] To avoid the deformation of practice into performance, she explains,

> Worship is erotic. The Beyoncé Mass does not worship Beyoncé, rather the multivalence of the Beyoncé Mass offers intimate space for uplifting contemporary Black women's music, literature and speech as sacred rhetoric to challenge the orthodoxy of the church using the everyday embodiment of Black women. In marrying this rhetoric to the erotic practice of worship the Beyoncé Mass uplifts the power and awe harnessed in Black women's bodies, agency, and sexuality.[93]

As erotic defiance suggests, the materiality of the erotic Black body in celebration of itself and its autonomy offers more than a counterargument to the idea of Black inferiority and the notion that Black bodies exist for the profit and pleasure of whiteness. It offers an experience that can be participated in. However, these experiences, like Black women's bodies, are sacred and must be protected and mediated when performed beyond the veil of Black women's intimate lives. It is under the sovereignty of each Black woman's pursuit of health and wholeness and the wisdom gleaned from the experience of their forebears that these boundaries should be drawn. For when these practices are made accessible to the perversions of capitalism's misogynoir, the beauty of Black sexuality is desecrated through exploitation. While these performances are seductive, offering forms of power and mobility, from an ethical perspective, guided by the erotic, they offer no true liberation without the power of the Spirit.

---

92 Personal interview with Yolanda Norton, March 3, 2023.
93 Norton interview.

CHAPTER FOUR

United in Death

Dying-in as a Posture of Solidarity

Then he said to me, "Prophesy to these bones, and say to them: O dry bones, hear the word of the Lord. Thus says the Lord God to these bones: I will cause breathe to enter you, and you shall live."

(Ezek 37:4–5)

The experience of the erotic resuscitates the will, emboldening the dispossessed to a responsibility for themselves once dislocated by oppression. A catalyst in the discovery and formation of Black women's unctuousness, the erotic—the manifestation and experience of love in and through the flesh—enables Black women to maintain the feistiness and tenacity that womanist ethicist Katie Cannon avers is necessary for them to survive their caustic environments.[1] This energy, I argue, fuels erotic defiance, a distinctive strategy of moral and political agency in which Black women and Black communities engage in an embodied praxis of resistance, self-definition, and world making. Black women's erotic defiance audaciously asserts authority over their bodies and resists their social regulation, commodification, and degradation. Rebelling against the assumed values and meanings of Black and female corporeality and the convoluted concept of the erotic operative in the fantasies of hegemonic imagination, erotic defiance is Black women's affirmation of their personhood, innate dignity and their refusal to submit to sinister significations and self-erasure, choosing instead to strain toward wholeness and self-actualization.

---

1 Cannon, *Black Womanist Ethics*, 104.

But what about other kinds of flesh? As chapter 1 argues, all of us are trapped in a system of significations that constrains our being and disciplines our behavior, even as we aspire to surmount it. But can non-Black people participate in erotic defiance? And, if so, how can those who are not Black avoid appropriating the ethic as just the latest episode in the long history of resources stolen from Black lives, bodies, and lands? Most relevant to the pursuit of Black liberation, can non-Black deployment of the strategy benefit the circumstances of Black people? This final chapter attempts to answer this question by positing erotic defiance as a posture of solidarity. In an age of social media activism, where virtue signaling is the standard tactic, the topic of solidarity has grown stale, particularly to Black people who watch as movements and corporations wanting to appear more progressive coopt the language of solidarity for the sake of appearing responsive to the plight of racial injustice for profits and clout. For many, solidarity has become synonymous with uninspiring declarations of sympathy and support that often lack the material dynamism to affect real change. Effectual solidarity, however, is an erotic practice.

To explore these questions and the erotic nature of effective solidarity, this chapter examines the ritual protest of "dying-in," a practice in which the flesh of protestors converges with the spirit of God to leverage the body's signifying and sacramental functions to offer a sacred counter-discourse in defense of Black life. Tracking the erotic in the call and response of Black death and the erotic defiance of the die-in, I contend that the erotic, as the energy that bonds human flesh and spirit one to the other, is the foundation of authentic solidarity, an effect of the corporeal mutuality of shared breath, mission, and vulnerability, and an embodied practice of kenosis.

THE CALL OF THE DEAD

The brutalized Black body—killed, beaten, robbed of its subjecthood—is a constant feature of American discourse and a perpetual assault on the psyches of Black Americans. According to a *Washington Times* database, of the thousand or more people killed by police in 2021, 22 percent were Black, despite Black citizens accounting for only 13 percent of the population.[2] Videos of

---

2 Washington Post staff, "Police Shootings Database 2015–2023: Search by Race, Age, Department," *Washington Post*, last modified May 25, 2023, https://www.washingtonpost.com/graphics/investigations/police-shootings-database/.

these shootings have made modern-day Black snuff films commonplace, haphazardly passed like notes between students in class across the interweb.[3]

After the tragic murder of Trayvon Martin and his killer's acquittal gripped the attention of the nation in 2013, sightings of Black death in mainstream and social media increased greatly. With every instance of violence, the watching Black community has been victimized as well. As Black writer Richard Wright laments in his novel *Black Boy*, "I had never in my life been abused by whites, but I had already become conditioned to their existence as though I had been the victim of a thousand lynchings."[4] Modern Black Americans undergo this psychic conditioning as indirect, interpersonal casualties of extrajudicial racialized violence. Stories of state violence against Black people assault us through detailed accounts of the annihilation of Black flesh, complete with live video footage. Over time, despite their ubiquity on social media, many of us, for the reasons of health, have developed the wisdom to abstain from the spectacle of Black death.

Despite or perhaps because of the dis-ease these sightings produce, the bodies of murdered Black people are unrivaled in moving communities to action against racial injustice. It is not a coincidence that the civil rights movement of the 1960s and the emergence of the Movement for Black Lives in 2013/14 were motivated by the showcasing of the bodies of two Black young men, more than fifty years apart. The first was Emmett Till, a fourteen-year-old Black boy visiting Mississippi from Chicago, accused of whistling at a white woman and speaking to her in a sexually familiar tone (the accuser, Joy Bryant, recanted the allegations more than forty years later). As a consequence for disrespecting a white woman, fourteen-year-old Till was abducted from his aunt's and uncle's home—literally ripped out of bed in the middle of the night—beaten beyond recognition, and thrown into the Tallahatchie River. When Till was later funeralized, his mother Mammie laid his mutilated body in an open casket for all the world to see, sparking national outrage among the Black community and beyond. This moment of intersubjective empathy is often described as the spark that initiated the movement.

More than fifty years after the lynching of Emmett Till, in Ferguson, Missouri, Michael Brown, a young Black man, was shot several times and killed

---

3 Phil Allen, *The Prophetic Lens: The Camera and Black Moral Agency* (Minneapolis: Fortress, 2022).

4 Richard Wright, *Black Boy*, 75th anniversary ed. (New York: HarperCollins, 2020), Kindle loc. 74.

by Officer Darren Wilson as he fled the scene after stealing cigars from a store unarmed. Like Till, Brown's murdered body was also displayed for all the world to see. This time, the exposure of the body was a product of the neglect of the Ferguson Police, who left Brown's body uncovered for more than four hours, emotionally and psychologically tormenting the all-Black neighborhood and the Black public who watched at home.

These sights of disregard for and desecration of Black life in America cast these bodies, trampled over by racialized violence, as signs of the perduring legacy of white domination. Yet these bodies have another affect. Like the blood of Abel, the bodies of murdered Black people cry out for justice (Gen 4:10). Those of us who identify with these victims, who recognize we too bear the mark that incites such violence, can hear the call of these victims not merely through the spectacle of the screen, but in a spiritual register. Black ourselves, we are haunted by the bodies of these victims, hyperaware of what seems to be the utter imperviousness of America's system of white domination, and of the chilling fact that the next dead Black person on the screen could just as easily be one of us.

Blackness provides a sense of corporeal mutuality with these victims, connecting those who identify as Black in love, grief, and excruciating vulnerability. Extrajudicial violence affects us haptically. The suffering it produces touches the lives of Black communities and affects even those African Americans who can evade violent encounters with police because of their intimate connections with others who might not have been so lucky. Black women especially must wrestle with the grief of seeing those they have birthed and nurtured as infants struck down with impunity. Sisters, aunties, and cousins, who have shared the tenderness of braiding hair, feeding bellies, and tending to bumps and scratches, and Black neighborhoods, otherwise known as extended family, that prove kinship exceeds the boundaries of blood—those who have scolded, encouraged, and protected victims like their own—are forced to grapple with the senseless injustice of the sting- ing absence of those they loved and continue to love even in death. This shared life contributes to the corporeal mutuality of Black experience—an experience of abundant love, but so too a torturous nagging in the wake of our awareness of our vulnerability to violence and even death, a mutuality that stifles the lives of the living.

My identification with the victims of extrajudicial violence began in the 1990s, first with the NYPD's sexual assault of Abner Luima with a plunger, and then the killing of Amadou Diallo, whose body was riddled with forty bullets. The egregious nature of the Diallo case sent my parents in a fury to marches and political protests calling for justice in New York City. I was too young to fully understand the implications of what had transpired. I knew both had been victimized because of racism, but the vulnerability of my own body and the haphazard nature of extrajudicial violence did not become real to me until much later with the death of Sandra Bland.

Bland was a twenty-eight-year-old Black woman who worked in higher education, like myself, in Prairie View, Texas, and was stopped for failing to signal. Self-possessed in ways often considered dangerous, Bland did not demonstrate the necessary deference to the authority of the officer, Brian Encina. She did not hold her tongue when he stopped her, nor did she conceal her irritation with him. Her unwillingness to bow to the officer's authority and her knowledge of her rights, which Bland asserted while Encina questioned her, surely antagonized him. The encounter then escalated with Encina ripping Bland out of her car and arresting her with force typically reserved for violent men. Throughout Encina's manhandling of Bland, she never relented from chastening Encina with threats to sue and mocking his manhood in the midst of his unwarranted violence against her, a woman. After being handcuffed, dragged, and thrown to the pavement, Bland was taken into custody. She was later found hanging by a garbage bag in her holding cell. According to police, her death was a suicide, a claim her friends and family vehemently reject.

While the body of Sandra Bland was not exposed to the public post-mortem, like Emmett's and Michael's, visions of her body torn from her car and tossed about like a rag doll haunt me nonetheless. The images of her body flailing join the chorus of flesh made corpses by those mandated to protect and serve. They expose the fallacy of the safety and security I imagine for myself as an educated, accomplished Black, because when I see the fate of Sandra Bland, I see myself. A Black female, a bit hot-headed at times, with a tongue that could make you wish she would have just gone ahead and hit you. Bland sassed the officer. Her emotions ran hot, and her mouth ran long. While many would offer this act of recalcitrance as an excuse for Encina's violence, womanist M. Shawn Copeland describes sass as a means of self-defense. "The use of mother wit and verbal dexterity to resist insult or assault," sass "denotes impudent, uppity speech; sharp, cutting back talk . . . thrown at the back."[5] Perceived by Copeland as a gift from African ancestors who found themselves captive in chattel slavery, sass enabled and enables Black women to engage in verbal warfare as a means of preserving their self-respect and self-authorization in moments of powerlessness. Providing Black women "the psychological distance to tell the truth," sass is a feature of Black women's survival and resistance.[6] Bland's truth was a poison to Encina, reminiscent of the bark of the poisonous West African sassy tree, from which the word derives its meaning.[7] Her words brought no physical harm to Encina, but they rhetorically obliterated his ego and authority. In a scenario where Bland had no rights beyond what Encina would allow, sass was her ready defense, allowing her to "return a portion of the poison the master."[8] But in this contest for authority, Bland was left battered, arrested, and ultimately dead.

Our racial identification with these victims weds us erotically to one another. They prompt an urging within the depths of our being to stand up for one another. In the same ways Amadou's body called my parents to action from the pages of the newspaper, the story of Sandra's death, the body of Michael Brown lying for hours on the news, and the sight of Eric Garner's and George Floyd's dying bodies called me to action as well. But in the streets of Nashville and the campus of Vanderbilt University, the site of most of my protest efforts, it was clear the humanity of these victims and the absence of justice called out to Black and non-Black alike, meeting us where the affective, flesh, and Spirit converge.[9] The call of the dead united us, connecting us beyond skin color or hair texture, through the mutual fear of the of inevitability of our human mortality, our sense of pathos for the dying. The heinous nature of these deaths mocks our fantasy of justice and

---

5 M. Shawn Copeland, "A Thinking Margin: The Womanist Movement as Critical Cognitive Praxis," in Floyd-Thomas, *Deeper Shades of Purple*, 233.

6 Copeland, "A Thinking Margin," 233.

7 Copeland, "A Thinking Margin," 233.

8 Copeland, "A Thinking Margin," 233.

9 Much has been written about the affective; in fact people often conflate my concept of the haptic with the affective. In my opinion this is a misstep, as the affective focuses on emotion and its affect and fails to account for the responsibility of what happens to and in the body. Here my use of the affective attends to the emotions of sympathy, empathy, and mutuality produced by witnessing Black death. For more on affect, see Brian Masumi, *Politics of Affect* (Malden, MA: Polity, 2015).

freedom, gripping our collective being, producing a version of empathy that moves people to action, to protest, to activism.

THE EROTIC DEFIANCE OF DYING (IN)

In the 1970s, environmental activists developed a protest tactic known as the die-in. Comparable to the sit-in made popular by the various movements that commanded American attention in the 1960s,[10] die-ins are a form of nonviolent social protest (action) that operate as social dramas and a site of contestation over the political and moral structure of a society.[11] Leveraging the dynamism of the body as a catalyst of economic and social disruption, protestors lie on the ground in public spaces as though dead to call attention to the normalization of death and injustice fomented by unethical environmental policies. AIDS activists later utilized the strategy in the '80s. Their bodies on the ground represented the many whose deaths by HIV/AIDS were ignored so not to trouble a false "Pax Americana" found in spaces of privilege, declaring peace where there is no peace.

In the nascence of the Movement for Black Lives,[12] begun in the wake of the spate of police shootings of unarmed Black people (Rekia Boyd, Michael

---

10 The sit-in is a form of social protest that aims to promote political, social, and/or economic changes. The technique, introduced by union activist and civil rights worker Bernice Fisher, uses the tactic of disruption of public and government space for the purposes of keeping issues of injustice at the forefront of American consciousness. For more on the sit-in, see M. J. O'Brien, *We Shall Not Be Moved: The Jackson Woolworth's Sit-In and the Movement It Inspired* (Jackson: University of Mississippi Press, 2013).

11 For more on the history of the die-in, see Deborah B. Gould, *Moving Politics: Emotion and ACT UP's Fight against AIDS* (Chicago: University of Chicago Press, 2009); and Victor Turner, *From Ritual to Theatre: The Human Seriousness of Play* (New York: PAJ, 1982), 9–11. Here I am alluding to Turner's concept of social drama and breach and repair. Turner describes social dramas as times of cultural and societal turbulence that can function as "a unit of description and analysis" that "revealed the 'taxonomic' relations among actors" (9). At this time, a community or society experiences a breach, or disruption in agreed-upon moral expectations. The social drama includes both the breach and the resolution of said breech, known as "repair."

12 The Black Lives Matter movement is a social action movement created by Alicia Garza et al. It was initially intended to garner attention for the all-but-ignored tradition of state-sanctioned violence against Black communities and the killing of unarmed Black men and women. The movement later expanded its focus to attend to the civil rights of Black people in general and the various injustices that contribute to Black oppression,

Brown, Eric Garner, and Jessica Williams), there was a resurgence of the protest strategy as people from all walks of life began to stand up for justice by lying down in solidarity with Black victims. Amid chants of "Hands up. Don't shoot"[13] and "I can't breathe," the bodies of protestors from various socioeconomic, racial, and cultural backgrounds stood as prophetic symbols and agents of disruption. They compromised the flow of goods and services in spaces of commerce such as malls, sporting events, and even busy thoroughfares. They interrupted the dignified beauty of elite college campuses and public institutions, symbolizing the corpses of America's despised—Black men and women, Black boys and girls slain by racialized, extrajudicial violence.

In the Longworth Building cafeteria on Capitol Hill, for example, an area described as heavily trafficked during lunch hours, about twenty-one clergy members shouted, "Black Lives Matter!" and proceeded to lie down on the floor, obstructing the path to the cash registers.[14] In the moments that passed, many others, including congressmen and -women, joined the clergy on the floor, lying down as though dead in symbolic protest. On their bodies were signs that said, "Black Lives Matter!" The *Washington Post* reported that the protest suspended the busy lunch rush in the cafeteria while diners and employees looked on, some proud of the statement that was being made.[15] The police soon came, threatening to arrest participants and ending what was intended to be a four-and-a-half-minute protest (typically used by protestors in memory of the four-and-a-half hours Michael Brown's body was left lying in the street) at three minutes.[16] At the close of the protest, clergy walked out singing, believing that their act of resistance would effectuate political change.

The protest ritual of the die-in exemplifies erotic defiance as a posture of solidarity. This form of erotic defiance is enacted through the leveraging of one's body in representation and identification with those made vulnerable

including poverty, unemployment, food scarcity, and other issues that disproportionately affect Black people. For more on the Black Lives Matter movement, see Keeanga-Yamahtta Taylor, *From #Black Lives Matter to Black Liberation* (Chicago: Haymarket, 2016).

13 The chant "Hands up. Don't shoot" was meant to call attention to the eyewitness account that Michael Brown, eighteen, had his hands up when police officer Darren Wilson shot him six times. "I can't breathe" represents the last words of Eric Garner as he was choked to death by police officer Daniel Pantaleo. Both are used to emphasize the lack of human regard with which police confront Black people suspected of committing a crime.

14 Wesley Lowery, "Black Lives Matter Protestors Stage Protest on Capitol Hill," *Washington Post*, January 21, 2015.

15 Lowery, "Black Lives Matter Protestors."

16 Lowery, "Black Lives Matter Protestors."

as a result of their Blackness. Through the erotic defiance of the die-in, protestors' bodies become sites of disruption, calling to account the systems of mass injustice that produce Black death. In this way, the bodies of protestors take on a prophetic function, serving as signs like the locusts sent to Egypt in the book of Exodus to warn an arrogant pharaoh of God's coming wrath (Ex 10:13–16), or the body of Isaiah, who preached naked to communicate the impending captivity of Israel (Isa 2:1–4). In the case of extrajudicial violence, the erotic defiance of the die-in interjects a sacred counter-discourse to what presents itself as the finality of the haptic discourse of white domination.

Offering a ritual praxis of Athanasius's assertion that "what is not assumed is not healed," the solidarity of the die-in relies on the centrality of the physical body in racist oppression, and the importance of the corporeal as the locus of metaphysical change for all humanity and God. Within this schema, the flesh serves as the site of healing encounter between God and human beings, disclosing the physical body's role as the arbiter of concrete reality.[17] Prioritizing the involvement of the flesh in the love we profess for those who suffer, the erotic defiance of dying-in talks back at the hegemonic forces of anti-Blackness, rejecting the racialized dynamics of engagement and threatening the social order as it pertains to certain kinds of bodies with the signifying power of protestors' own physical bodies. A fleshy practice of bodies together in one time, place, and space, moving together, or in this case lying in heaps with one another in solidarity with the slain, the erotic defiance of dying-in requires an intentional leaning in to a contrary or divine economy that acknowledges the sovereignty of God, the sacred value of Black life, and the union we all share through God's breath.

EROTIC DEFIANCE AS SACRED COUNTERDISCOURSE

In his debut book *Black Pentecostal Breath*, Black studies scholar Ashon Crawley suggests the haunting plea "I can't breathe," uttered by Eric Garner, the Black man choked to death by New York City police in 2014, is a

---

17 Athanasius, *On the Incarnation*, trans. Penelope Lawson (Crestwood, NY: St. Vladimir's Seminary Press, 1998), 12. Athanasius asserts the incarnation is the beginning of God's saving work in Jesus Christ. Through the incarnation, divinity assumes humanity through the act of assuming flesh for the sake of redeeming it. Athanasius writes, "For the solidarity of mankind is such that, by virtue of the Word's indwelling in a single human body, the corruption which goes with death has lost its power overall."

call or charge "to do something, to perform, to produce otherwise than we have . . . to be caught up in the cause against violence."[18] This plea, indeed, called us, the witnesses of this gross display of inhumanity, to responsibility; however, I contend this plea does not stop with the verbal cries of victims. Rooted in the breath of Garner's existence, his plea continues as the breath that unites us and beckons us to action. According to the biblical record in Genesis, humanity's story begins with God's breath. Breathing life into the dust formed from the ground, God made humans living beings. Without this breath, life is not possible. None of humanity's vitality, creativity, nor its existence is possible apart from the breath of God. The breath of God, shared between us, which called and breathed creation into being, makes life sacred and binds us in life-giving love to the divine Creator and each other. But what happens when this breath is extinguished as it was in the case of Eric Garner, or Sandra Bland? Does it snuff out the love that unites Black victims with God and their human kin? No, most certainly not. The breath of God and its erotic impulse call out, troubling the flesh of those who remain to respond with action.

In her book *Enfleshing Freedom*, M. Shawn Copeland weds solidarity to the body. Describing solidarity as a set of bodily practices that within a Christian schema provide relational service to and for others for the benefit of the kindom of God, she argues solidarity not only involves the concrete practice of love in our relationships with the other, but also requires the service of our flesh as a spiritual witness of our allegiance to God and God's truth and justice. When effectively practiced, solidarity, according to Copeland, follows in the practice of Jesus, who offered his own flesh as a way to shoulder and overcome that which oppresses humanity. In other words, fleshy acts of service toward our fellow human unite the practitioner with the Spirit of Christ who suffered, as well as those who suffer in our present age. More than just a bodily practice, Copeland's concept of Christian solidarity is erotic in nature. Through it, God and flesh converge through acts of love and humanity and are knit together as one in loving service and relationship to one another. But too often the privileged believe that money or an antiracism training will sufficiently satisfy a posture of solidarity. Effectual solidarity, however, demands more than bodily acts, but a corporeal mutuality made possible through shared breath, mission, and experiences of identification.

---

18 Ashon Crawley, *Black Pentecostal Breath: The Aesthetics of Possibility* (New York: Fordham University Press, 2016), 1–2.

The shared nature of God's breath between humanity, I argue, is the founding principle of the erotic nature of solidarity. It can be seen in the Black church as the spirit of God moves, as Black church folk say, "from heart to heart and breast to breast." The movement of the Holy Spirit from one to the other is captured in Jarena Lee's experience of prophetic utterance. One of the first Black female preachers in American history, Lee recounts that when she was in church one day listening to a sermon, the Spirit left the preacher, Rev. Richard Williams, in the midst of his sermon, and "in the same instant" impelled her to exhort, suggesting that the spirit that vacated Williams and emboldened her speak were one and the same.[19]

Karen Baker-Fletcher describes the movement of the Spirit as the breath of God, or *ruach* in the Hebrew.[20] It is by this breath that God creates the universe and animates humanity to life. It is by this Spirit or breath that that divine proclamation is possible. Lee's description of Williams's loss of "the Spirit" can be likened to the loss of the breath of God: that which gave him the capacity for divine proclamation had been stunted. Yet what is remarkable and relevant to this project is the way that same Spirit or breath rises up in Lee, such that she is able to resuscitate divine breath, life, and energy in that moment for the worshipping community through her own prophetic speech acts. While Lee's response to the call was to preach, the response of the community to the call of the dying and dead involves a similar sacred discourse. Both engage in prophetic proclamation—divine communication on behalf of Spirit and flesh.

Likewise, the bodies of Trayvon Martin, Michael Brown, Sandra Bland, Amadou Dialo, and Eric Garner call to those who remain. This plea of the dying is not silenced by death. As philosopher of religion Biko Mandela Gray writes, "Flesh vibrates beyond the opposition of life and death. And perhaps because it does, these lives still speak. They can still be heard. Perhaps it is this possibility of being heard that speaks to flesh's religious capacities too."[21] I contend that the affective chorus of corpses and their effect on the living disclose the religious capacity of the flesh as an erotic one, giving flesh and even bodies whose breath has been snuffed out the ability to beckon us closer in sacred union.

---

19 Jarena Lee, *Preaching with Sacred Fire*, ed. Martha Simmons (New York: W. W. Norton, 2010), 162.

20 Karen Baker-Fletcher, *Dancing with God: The Trinity from a Womanist Perspective* (St. Louis: Chalice Press, 2006), 54.

21 Biko Mandela Gray, *Black Life Matter: Blackness, Religion, and the Subject* (Durham, NC: Duke University Press, 2022), 27.

Contrary to the world's conflation of the erotic with sexual desire, Baker-Fletcher describes eros as desire for union with the sacred."[22] By sacred, Baker-Fletcher means "the depth, breath, integrity and energy of all that God has created.... Eros," she argues, "seeks spiritual depth."[23] Of the many definitions feminists and womanists offer for the erotic, Baker-Fletcher's emphasis on sacred union provides a key for understanding the impulse that connects the brutalized victims of extrajudicial violence with those who remain. Describing the connection between the living and the dead as erotic may initially feel inappropriate; however, it resonates when we consider how humanity's shared breath with the divine calls us together as one. This, I argue, is the essential work of the erotic.

Said energy is not relegated to the fomenting of sexual desire or selfish pleasure, but is the very spirit that unites humans and God as one. Crawley would shun the idea of categorizing this breath in Western theological conceptions of God. Still, for those who rely on such categories, his account of breath is strikingly similar to womanist accounts of the erotic life of the Holy Spirit. Given Crawley's locus of investigation, the sensual, affective, and material performances of what Black Pentecostals would call Holy Spirit–possessed flesh, this is unsurprising.[24] The Pentecostal tradition's pneumatology follows the early church's theology of the performance of the Spirit and ecclesiology. Theirs was a tradition of Africanity and familiarity with the Spirit world. As ethicist Cheryl Sanders explains in her treatment of Black Holiness and Pentecostal traditions, converts understood their flesh to be possessed and controlled by the Spirit; in similar ways to Candomblé and voudou, however, diverging from other spiritualities that featured spirit possession, Pentecostal and Holiness churches, who staunchly maintained the oneness of God, believed that to be "possessed by the Spirit" was to be given wholly over specifically and "exclusively" to the Holy Ghost, the third person of the triune God, for God's use.[25]

Regardless of how this dynamism is described, these modes of spiritual/material being stand in defiance to the hegemonic modes of living and relationality of a secular society. They interrupt traditional—what Black

---

22 Baker-Fletcher, "The Erotic in Contemporary Black Women's Writings," 202.

23 Baker-Fletcher, "The Erotic in Contemporary Black Women's Writings," 202.

24 Crawley, *Black Pentecostal Breath*, 37.

25 Cheryl Sanders, *Saints in Exile: The Holiness-Pentecostal Experience in African American Religion and Culture* (New York: Oxford University Press, 1996), 59.

Pentecostals would call "worldly"—modes of living for practices that render participants peculiar yet powerful. Crawley describes this breath as the invincible, ongoing sound of movement toward freedom that cannot and will never be stilled, a sonic event inhabited in flesh, that constitutes selfhood, a description that shares great similarity with progenitor of womanist ethics Katie Cannon's principal virtue of unctuousness as that which affirms selfhood in Black women in the face of incredible odds.[26] Crawley argues this breath or vibration shared by all human beings is indomitable, disruptive, and always moving toward liberation. While Crawley locates this breath or vibration in sound, I situate it firmly in the erotic activity of God.

The breath of God present in the pleas of the dying functions haptically on those who remain. As these pleas vacate the body, choking out of Garner the last of that which constitutes life, they speak. They haunt. They provoke. As Gray argues, these lives speak beyond death, moving the flesh of those who remain to action, to defense on the victim's behalf. If Crawley is correct that Garner's plea, "I can't breathe," was a charge to live otherwise, or in opposition to violence, then the erotic defiance of dying-in is a response of the defiant to that call. Living through a relentless culture of Black death that seems inextinguishable, die-in protests were a striking reminder of how many had not bowed the knee to Baal (1 Kgs 19:18), that there were still many who longed for an otherwise reality.[27] Their offerings of solidarity served as prophetic rituals, disrupting the quotidian nature of Black death in the United States with a sacred counterdiscourse in which the breath of God spoke back through all kinds of flesh for the victims of extrajudicial violence. Just as Sandra Bland sassed the officer in their violent encounter, the die-in's prophetic assertions of the sacrality of Black life sass hegemonic powers, mocking their authority as the final word on what can and will be.

Bodies, their presentation and their activity in the world, have creative power, according to secular humanist Anthony Pinn. He contends that that they have the capacity to reframe notions of the religious, revealing what is perceived as virtuous and what is constructed as evil, what is valued and what is discarded as insignificant.[28] The protest of die-in vivifies Pinn's assertion,

---

26 Crawley, *Black Pentecostal Breath*, 6.

27 Here I use the language of "otherwise" in accord with Crawley's use in *Black Pentecostal Breath*. Crawley offers the term *otherwise* as an alternative to the language of "alternative" in the hopes of displacing the assumption of normativity on the reality of violence produced by anti-Blackness. For more, see Crawley, *Black Pentecostal Breath*, 1–2.

28 Pinn, *Embodiment and the New Shape*, xiii.

declaring not only Black life as significant, but Black people integral members of society, worthy of risky, fleshy representation. In this way, the bodies of protesters function as "material realities that shape information within the context of the world."[29] Acting as symbolic representatives, they have an effect on the worlds they live in.[30] Their activity has the capacity to materially ratify or contest socially constructed meanings assigned to them and to other bodies, as well as to contribute to or combat the oppressive circumstances that rely on these formulations as a result of bodies functioning as signifiers. Pinn, Copeland, and philosophers like Maurice Merleau-Ponty have long held that the physical body has an effect on the world it lives in. Functioning like a living organism, the social body, or a community's collective consciousness, absorbs concepts and messages that are integrated into commonly held understandings. These shifting meanings, which are perpetually reorienting the meanings of reality, make embodied solidarity a unique opportunity for cultural and moral transformation for the individual and the community.[31]

Activated by the erotic breath of God that coheres victim, God, and survivors together, protestors in the loving mutuality of shared breath and mission declare the sanctity of Black life with the material weight of their own bodies. This process by which the bodies of murdered Black victims call out to the living and the prophetic response of the die-in can be understood as a resuscitation of the lives and voices of the slain, comparable to Ezekiel and the valley of dry bones. Life is breathed back into these dry bones, void of life, through acts of prophecy—the sacred counterdiscourse of God. Though the bones showed no sign of life, the word of God said, "I will cause breath to enter you, and you shall live" (Ezek 37:4–5). As a result, bones that were once disconnected are joined back together, life springs forth, and they stand on their feet as an army. Likewise, though the extrajudicial violence and neglect of the American justice system offered only a report of death, the breath of God active in the works of the flesh of protestors resuscitates the voice of the dead. It speaks back. Black Lives Matter cofounder Patrisse Marie Khan-Cullors Brignac offers a perspective inflected with African spirituality, arguing the work of protest, resistance, and spreading awareness is like "resurrecting a spirit so they can

---

29 Pinn, *Embodiment and the New Shape*, xiii.

30 Pinn, *Embodiment and the New Shape*, xiii. For more, see Harrod, *Human Center*; and Copeland, introduction to *Enfleshing Freedom*.

31 For more on the construction of meaning and the perpetually shifting values of the body and reality, see Harrod, *Human Center*; and Sokolowski, *Moral Action*.

work through us."[32] While Cullors would describe this spirit as the spirit of the victim, from a Christian perspective, I contend it is the shared breath of God, or the erotic nature of the Holy Spirit that is present in this work. More than symbolic, the die-in is prophetic. It fosters and is fostered by this spirit. It speaks back to the powers that would attempt to exalt themselves above God and forges potential pathways to solidarity.[33]

MUTUALITY IN DEATH

Theologian and mystic Howard Thurman writes of the sense of solidarity enslaved Black people felt with Jesus on account of an experience of identification. Jesus's experiences of being apprehended, tortured, and ultimately killed in the undignified way many Black Americans have been killed made him someone enslaved Blacks could connect with. They believed Jesus could meet them in their unique sufferings. They were confident that Jesus understood the direness of the mortifying violence they faced and could shoulder the burden with them, and even act on their behalf. They found fellowship with Jesus in his humiliation, suffering, and death and because of this mutuality, his resurrection as well, amplifying the importance of corporeal mutuality in the work of solidarity.

The pursuit of mutuality is a principle aim of the erotic. Feminist theologian Carter Heyward writes, "The erotic is our embodied yearning for mutuality . . . a desire for something we don't have yet," but is something we must work to achieve.[34] One of the ways we work toward mutuality with the divine and with others is through the giving of ourselves in the service of others. In so doing we accomplish mutuality, as Copeland argues, with Jesus, a mutuality comprised of concrete acts of love to communities and individuals who suffer.[35] So too, as protestors take up the cause of those who suffer

---

32 Alejandra Molina, "Black Lives Matter Is 'a Spiritual Movement,' Says Co-Founder Patrisse Cullors," Religion News Service, June 15, 2020, https://religionnews.com/2020/06/15/why-black-lives-matter-is-a-spiritual-movement-says-blm-co-founder-patrisse-cullors/.

33 Crawley, *Black Pentecostal Breath*, 2.

34 Carter Heyward, *Touching Our Strength: The Erotic as Power and the Love of God* (San Francisco: HarperCollins, 1989), 105.

35 Douglas, *What's Faith Got to Do with It?*, 67. Douglas explains demonized difference as a religious and cultural phenomenon, influenced by platonic dualism in which difference is automatically perceived as dangerous, necessitating its expulsion for the safety of the community.

in and through practices of their own flesh, they offer concrete manifestations of love in their flesh or eros for the oppressed. They make their bodies a spectacle in identification with the bodies of the murdered, such that they cannot be silenced. Further, they render their bodies vulnerable through acts of identification and mutuality. Dying-in, after all, requires one lay lifeless, typically in a busy thoroughfare or place of commerce, vulnerable to disciplining forces. As agitators of the status quo, people willing to enact allegiance with the despised through their own embodied agency model an alternative way of being in the world, their bodies taking on the same kind of status and vulnerability as the oppressed. They become sites of contestation between the hegemonically orchestrated consciousness of the dominant culture, and a consciousness oriented by justice and solidarity. So too, they represent a threat to the prevailing powers. As representatives of the oppressed and the spirit of truth and justice, the bodies of participants represent bodies out of order—bodies engaged in the disruption of white privilege and power—and must therefore be disciplined.

Heather Hayer was the victim of such disciplining in August 2017 in Charlottesville, Virginia, when a white supremacist, enraged by protesters' display of allegiance to Black and brown people, plowed into a crowd of activists, killing her and injuring many more. The bodily vulnerability of protestors is an inescapable reality. The Freedom Summer murders of James Chaney, Andrew Goodman, and Michael Schwerner in 1964 attest to the fact that individuals committed to the maintenance of white supremacy will kill their own in its pursuit. These dangers become more pronounced as stories increase of people running cars into protests and of self-deputized actors like Kyle Rittenhouse, who came to a protest in Kenosha, Wisconsin, armed and ready to engage in tactical combat. Despite his traveling across state lines with a gun he was too young to purchase, America's justice system was unwilling to find Rittenhouse culpable when he killed two people and injured another in his clash with protestors, thereby sanctioning this kind of violence for future vigilantes. In addition to the threat of death, protestors make themselves vulnerable to assault at the hands of the police and the public. They also render themselves subject to arrest. These dangers mimic, albeit fleetingly, the vulnerability of Black Americans, fostering a mutuality fomented by violence and death.

In her book *Religious Resistance to Neoliberalism*, ethicist Keri Day posits that the neoliberal rationale, operative in our political economy, foments a passionless, disconnected posture in the world as a means of survival and economic flourishing.[36] As a mindset and mode of sociality informed by white patriarchy and capitalism, the neoliberal rationale compels people to relate competitively rather than cooperatively.[37] The influence of the neoliberal rationale, Day argues, is expansive. It orders our sociality, our customs, and our ethics—all too often it demands what Black feminist writer Audre Lorde would describe as a pornographic mode of relationality in which people exploit others for the purposes of their own gain and/or are exploited themselves. As a result, neoliberal approaches foment a dynamic of domination that causes many, especially those marginalized by bodily difference, to experience alienation from their sense of humanity as various economic systems separate them from their creativity, self-possession, and passions.

In the Lordean tradition,[38] Day argues that the erotic challenges passionless and numb ways of being encouraged by the neoliberal rationale.[39] Lorde suggests that for those struggling with the oppressive forces of racist patriarchy (which would include the marginalized and the privileged), numbness often feels like "the only alternative."[40] However, the political power of the erotic exists in its ability to inspire confrontation of and resistance to deleterious pornographic modes of relation inspired by greed and a lust for power. In Lorde's words, "In touch with the erotic, I become less willing to accept powerlessness, or those other supplied states of being which are not native to me, such as resignation, despair, self-effacement."[41] The erotic informs and illuminates our engagement in the world around us. It radicalizes us by locating and connecting us to our humanity, our will, and our worth. Identifying our deepest feelings, it inspires us to reject anemic, dispossessed, despondent ways of being in the world and instills a sense of self-worth, power, defiance, hope, joy, and pleasure.

Awakening individuals to their humanity, "the erotic inspires a wealth of alternatives to a state of numbness and disconnectedness."[42] It restores our humanity by reviving the power of our flesh—our relational being. Reviving

---

36 Day, *Religious Resistance to Neoliberalism*, 98.

37 Day, *Religious Resistance to Neoliberalism*, 4.

38 This signifies the tradition of rereading the erotic by Audre Lorde, which has become quite popular in African American studies.

39 Day, *Religious Resistance to Neoliberalism*, 98.

40 Lorde, "Uses of the Erotic," 58.

41 Lorde, "Uses of the Erotic," 58.

42 Courtney Bryant Prince, "Erotic Defiance: A Womanist Ethic of Moral and Political Agency" (PhD diss., Vanderbuilt University, 2018), 102.

us from disassociated relationality, the erotic reconnects us to the bodies societal institutions continually encourage us to forget and makes known the way to ethical living that privileges the humanity of others and our relationships with them. Ushering us into a liberated mode of existence in which we feel and feel deeply, connect with others, and are aware of our divine right to freedom, the erotic enables us to discern and challenge the absence of mutuality in "hierarchical relationships sponsored by oppressive regimes like racism, neoliberalism, sexism, etc."[43] Further, the erotic cultivates a sense of responsibility, which incites action.[44] It inspires us to transgress the societal boundaries that systems of capitalism, racism, and patriarchy have installed and to challenge their legitimacy.

Day contends that the erotic is a resource for ethical living that moves us beyond abstractions or the theoretical, to an understanding of the concrete ways in which oppression compromises one's humanness, connections, and freedoms. In this way, erotic knowledge, as Lorde argues, connects the spiritual to the political through shared sensual, emotional, and psychic expressions. It, therefore, becomes a bridge, a point of encounter and connection capable of reconciling the estranged.[45] For example, within the context of extrajudicial violence against Black people, erotic knowledge moves beyond the abstract concept of order, crime, and obedience (societal facets perennially invoked as responses to racialized violence) and sees the killing of unarmed men and women from the lens of kinship, like the perspectives of the families and communities affected. Surely the sense of connection to a young man lying dead in the street for hours, or the feelings associated with the loss of a family member to police violence or disproportionate incarceration, resonates in ways that statistics and theory cannot. The inclusion of the erotic in the work of solidarity signals the importance of the body in the manifestation of the concrete, especially in the case of love. Yet equally as important are experiences of identification.

Using the example of a mother sharing her concrete struggles with being present with her children and providing safety and fundamental resources for them in the midst of working a low-wage job, Day argues that erotic knowledge allows her audience to emotionally connect with the mother's situation. Through hearing of this mother's struggle, Day contends, the

---

43 Day, *Religious Resistance to Neoliberalism*, 98.
44 Lorde, "Uses of the Erotic," 58.
45 Lorde, "Uses of the Erotic," 56.

listeners have the opportunity for transformation, prompting others toward responsible action. She writes, "The erotic in this case sponsors connection that becomes the grounding for protest and political action."[46] Rather than as cultivating erotic knowledge, I would describe Day's example as one of intersubjective empathy. The audience that hears the mother's story encounters, or rather is confronted with, the concrete struggle of an individual with whom they can choose to commiserate and mobilize on behalf of as a fellow human being, or not. For many, encounters with these mothers have been transformational experiences, spurring them to join and fight against police violence and other abuses of Black people. Yet, true to the disconnected posture of Western civilization, countless mothers have shared their pain with the nation, via articles, stories, and rallies, only to be disregarded. I press Day's logic that the hearing of a story can produce the kind of connection that motivates us to "move toward each other in support of one's collective well-being."[47] My challenge is based on the way the erotic manifests love in the concrete through bodily participation. Day argues an affective politics allows the sentiments of love to inspire active commitments to particular political causes. However, in his work on affect, Brian Masumi argues that emotion of the affective is for the individual alone. In other words, it demands no responsibility to act.[48] The erotic, I argue, moves beyond sentiments to right relationality. Such movement, I contend, is inspired by experiences of corporeal mutuality.

Echoing philosopher Gabriel Marcel's premise that to understand suffering, it must touch you, Howard Thurman conveys the power of Jesus's kenotic acts of divesting himself of his power for the sake of mutuality with the vulnerable.[49] Apprehended, tortured, and ultimately lynched, Jesus suffered in the same ways as those rendered vulnerable by race. Thurman asserts that Jesus-on-the-cross operates as a quality of identification in experience with the crucified.[50] I would argue his life as a disenfranchised Jew, sharing in the struggle of the oppressed through the concrete experience of their vulnerability to oppressive political powers, is another manifestation of Jesus's

---

46 Day, *Religious Resistance to Neoliberalism*, 99.

47 Day, *Religious Resistance to Neoliberalism*, 99.

48 Masumi, *Politics of Affect*.

49 Gabriel Marcel, *The Philosophy of Existence*, trans. Manya Harari (Freeport, NY: Books for Libraries Press, 1969), 9.

50 Howard Thurman, *Deep River: An Interpretation of Negro Spirituals* (Whitefish, MT: Literary Licensing, 1945), 27, quoted in Douglas, *Stand Your Ground*, 178.

willingness to relinquish power for the sake of mutuality with, and ultimately liberation of, the oppressed.

These experiences demonstrate Jesus's eros—that is, shared bodily and sacrificial love for those who suffer—as a foundational element to the practice of solidarity. While Day acknowledges that love is a concrete practice, her account of the erotic fails to consider identification or mutuality. It is unrealistic to believe people will be inspired to take up the suffering of those they are not concretely familiar with. Americans' inaction toward the plight of its Black citizens suggests emotion as it is understood cannot be the impetus for just relations among strangers. In fact, many, though familiar with the emotional accounts of how lives and families have been devastated by the government's lack of regard for Black life, remain unaffected, continuing in the counterrhetoric of "All lives matter" and the notion that cooperation with the police will keep Black people safe. The differences in responses raise questions about empathetic encounters and their efficacy in generating erotic knowledge.

EROTIC SOLIDARITY AS A
KENOTIC POSTURE

I argue that embodied kenosis is a necessity for practicing solidarity. Through these experiences Jesus identifies with the exploited and their suffering in his flesh. Likewise, the act of dying-in, like other acts of solidarity, presents opportunities for the practice of the renunciation of privilege through bodily identification with the oppressed. Through exposure to the threat of the coercive technologies of the state, including arrest, violence, and even the threat of death that demonized communities experience daily, embodied performances of solidarity enable protestors to experience briefly the vulnerability of Black and poor communities. Participation in embodied resistance in solidarity with Black people allows those with privilege to be "touched by suffering," facilitating experiences of identification that model solidarity as a corporeal manifestation of love, mutuality, and the practice of womanist kenosis.

Distinct from the traditional doctrine of kenosis, womanist kenosis is a renunciation of one's privilege for the sake of the mutual sharing of power. Taking into account how the traditional doctrine of kenosis has been deployed as the theological justification for the dispossession of the bodies and agency of women, especially Black women, womanist theologians like Delores Williams and Marcia Riggs have contested the merit of an ethic of sacrifice that offers no relief from the hierarchical relationality that degrades and suppresses Black women's freedom.[51] Reinterpreting kenosis as the relinquishing of power, privilege, and exceptionalism in the pursuit of the mutual sharing of power, womanist theological scholars like theologian Kelly Brown Douglas have expanded the social implications of kenosis, making it relevant to the moral situation of Black women specifically, and Black people in general.[52]

Douglas demystifies the kenosis of Jesus on the way to the cross, contextualizing its implications in concrete reality. She argues, "Jesus empties himself not only of his divinity, but his worldly status."[53] Refusing to respond or advocate for himself in any way, he renounces any sense of power or privilege he possesses and chooses instead to identify with the despised by allowing his body to be subject to the violence of governmental and evil powers. Douglas's description points to the material and physical experience necessary in the forging of political solidarity. Jesus shares in the vulnerability of the oppressed by risking his own flesh. Through his refusal to shun experiences of marginalization, ridicule, and injustice, he is able to truly identify with the vulnerable in the flesh. As such, he models the erotic nature of solidarity as a concrete practice of love and corporeal mutuality, which requires a renunciation of privilege and encounters of vulnerability.

Douglas's characterization of solidarity exceeds warm sentiments and even pleasure and desire and underscores our responsibility to one another. Echoing Lorde, the erotic demands from us excellence.[54] Excellence, however, is not easy. It requires a sense of disciplined responsibility and even sacrifice. Like the passion of Jesus, and in the case of embodied ritual protests like die-ins,

---

51 Black women's bodies, being, and personhood were seen as instruments of sexual pleasure and economic profit: first by white people, then Black men, and finally the Black community at large. Under the auspices of Christian obedience, Black women have been spiritually coerced into making themselves small as a way of following in the service and suffering of Christ. Ignoring their own needs for survival, suppressing their personhood, and living for the service of others, they have been the victims of a society hell-bent on their exploitation. For more on the death-dealing ethic of sacrifice operative in Black women's Christian communities, see Walker-Barnes, *Too Heavy a Yoke*; and Delores Williams, *Sisters in the Wilderness: The Challenge of Womanist God-Talk* (Maryknoll, NY: Orbis, 2013).

52 Douglas, *Stand Your Ground*, 177; Riggs, *Awake, Arise & Act*, 94.

53 Douglas, *Stand Your Ground*, 177.

54 Lorde, "Uses of the Erotic," 55.

solidarity requires an embodied kenosis—a movement toward *corporeal* mutuality for the sake of solidarity with the oppressed. Enacted through the disciplined and risky renunciation of privilege, authority, and power, it highlights solidarity's accountability to the community. These efforts are not merely mystically symbolic acts of submission between protestors and the divine. They are sacrificial acts motivated by a desire for right relation with the oppressed, demonstrated through fleshy vulnerability, that is, embodied identification with the marginalized, pursued through *experiences of*, rather than *reflection on*, vulnerability and suffering, as witnessed in the passion of Jesus Christ. These experiences offer a metaphor for moral formation in which participants' vulnerability underscores the integral role of sacrifice in solidarity and political transformation. This kind of risk is not for the faint of heart.

Too many understand solidarity as sympathy for those who suffer, or standing with those who suffer, but Christ's solidarity takes up the suffering of Black people as his own. The cross and its experiences of identification with the vulnerable thus become the standard and criteria for the practice of solidarity. So too, protestors' experiences of corporeal mutuality with the vulnerable can provide a better understanding of the suffering of the other, moving the privileged to confront and address its oppressive cause and help them shoulder the burden.[55] Actualizing love for those who suffer from the abstract to the concrete, these embodied acts of protest are enfleshed manifestations of the solidarity with the oppressed the privileged profess.

Returning to the question of the possibility of non-Black people participating in erotic defiance—the embodied affirmation of the Black subject and its dignity—the answer is yes, for erotic defiance in non-Black people equates to an authentic posture of solidarity. As this chapter has argued, effectual solidarity is far more costly than Western discourse has suggested. Not only does it demand the participation of the body, but it entails risk to the body in pursuit of mutuality and identification with the racially despised. Said mutuality requires the bodily renunciation of privileges afforded on account of one's whiteness or proximity to whiteness like comfort, safety, peace. For many accustomed to these advantages, the renunciation of privilege and even the death of self required for mutuality will feel like loss. However, effectual solidarity includes following in the kenotic posture of Jesus and all the danger and vulnerability it produces. As such, it requires that participants renounce the ideologies and ethics that breathe life into their privilege.

---

55 Copeland, *Enfleshing Freedom*, 94.

Thus, I am arguing that to participate in the solidarity of erotic defiance, those who are not Black must learn to breathe differently, to act and identify in new ways. For the pornographic force that maintains the glorification of whiteness is not learned but inhaled. It is breathed into our consciousness as we exist. It is felt on our flesh in our haptic encounters; it is imposed upon our identities as we are diminished or exalted in an anti-Black world. To breathe differently is to privilege the breath of God that connects all living beings, rather than the spirit of domination that gives life to privilege born of the flesh. Renouncing the dynamics of domination that declare Black flesh evil, subordinate, and inferior, it imitates Jesus, who renounced his spiritual and worldly privilege so that humanity might be free and reconciled back unto God.

When power and privilege are renounced in concrete ways for the benefit of those with less power, we pursue mutuality with those who are more prone to suffering. In our modern culture, often we rely on touch—the temporary sharing of space and sensation—the haptic encounters as a shortcut to mutuality. However, kenosis, the renunciation of self and its power, which is required for solidarity, is actually the work necessary to make lasting mutuality a reality. Both methods can be erotic, as the erotic functions as a bridge unifying God and humanity, person to person, and even the disparate aspects of our singular lives like the rational and the emotional.

It cannot be emphasized enough that participation in the ritual of protest alone does not fulfill the full demand of Christian solidarity. The embodied rituals of solidarity inform believers' understanding of proper relationality with the oppressed, giving them a rubric of how to conduct themselves in concrete reality. It does not fulfill it. However, these acts have the potential to morally form those who participate. Through the ritual of dying-in, protesters acknowledge their connection to a social body that is made of diverse communities, perspectives, and experiences. This interconnectedness, funded by the mutuality of breath and ratified through shared mission and identification, demands justice for the oppressed with the same urgency with which one would pursue justice for oneself.

ESCAPING PRESCRIBED BOUNDARIES
OF THE EROTIC

The illumination of the erotic nature of solidarity, as disclosed in the erotic care of the soul, Black women's erotic dance, and the protest ritual of the die-in, reveals the expansive nature and function of the erotic beyond traditional categories of pleasure and desire, particularly its political dimensions. Disclosing the relationship between the erotic and sacrifice, this investigation of the die-in contributes to the ongoing womanist discourse on kenosis and the role of sacrifice in religio-ethical practice.

Embodied protest is an erotic endeavor of the body, made possible and effective through the sacrificial pursuit of mutuality in the manifestation of a materially demonstrated love of the bodies and beings of the oppressed. Still, sacrifice has oppressive connotations in womanist theology and ethics. Moreover, Western society's suppression and mischaracterization of the erotic has taken root in the psyche of the marginalized to such a degree that in our attempts to redeem the erotic, womanist and feminist scholars have neglected the erotic's role in seeking fullness and fulfillment in other kinds of human relationality.

However, human gratification and satisfaction are not limited to the sexual alone. In fact, erotiphobia's tendency to do so hinders our ability to see and enjoy the benefits of the truly expansive nature of the erotic. Attention to the expansive dimensions of the erotic orients us to the many modes of abundant living humanity was created for and its power for political transformation. The function of the erotic in authentic solidarity as seen in the protest ritual of the die-in discloses that its virtues extend beyond individual pleasure or desires. It promotes our sense of communal accountability, our responsibility, and our participation in the work of creativity in the world.

The debunking of the erotic as demonic and its embrace as a resource for moral agency contests the power of erotophobia over our personal and political freedoms. As Lorde argues, the erotic gives us access to the resource inside us that gives way to corporeal and relational power and agency, especially among those who are oppressed. Facilitating the fullness of our personhood through revelatory knowledge about ourselves and the world, the erotic also spurs personal and communal accountability. Hence, the erotic is a conscientizing and guiding agent of truth. Lorde writes, "It [the erotic] is an internal sense of satisfaction"—a fullness or sense of wholeness—"to which, once we have experienced it, we know we can aspire. For having experienced the fullness of this depth of feeling and recognizing its power, in honor and self-respect, we can require no less of ourselves."[56] Moving

---

56 Lorde, "Uses of the Erotic," 54.

us from mediocrity to excellence, the erotic reinvigorates our lives with passion, waking us from a strategy of numbness (the suppression of our humanness) for the sake of survival to a place of proactivity that challenges injustice and oppression.

The erotic as a divine resource of moral agency draws us toward one another, not only in a sexual or romantic capacity, but in solidarity as human beings and children of God. It is the desire for community, the impulse that moves us toward each other, the desire to know one another, to participate in one another's lives, to find home in each other. Eros animates deep engagement, not only with the bodies of the others, but with their hearts, minds, and spirits as well. This intimate engagement impels us to contest that which obstructs our coherence and communion with each other through various forms of erotic defiance—the concrete divestment of hegemonic conventions and their performance. Consequently, erotic defiance diverges from a focus on self and fully commits to the exchange, communion, and connection it accomplishes. When it does not, what was potentially initially prophetic and transformative devolves into the pornographic. Lorde's words are instructive. She writes, "To share the power of each other's feelings is different from using each other's feelings. When we look the other way," a metaphor for disconnected exchanges between individuals, "we use rather than share the feelings of those others who participate with us. . . . We use each other as objects of satisfaction rather than share joy in the satisfying."[57] Accordingly, the erotic demands mutuality. It is the reciprocal exchange of deep feelings, the energy produced in the pursuit of shared goals, in the sharing of experiences, as well as the impetus and energy to accomplish transformation in our world.

The erotic resuscitates our connection not only to ourselves, but to each other. As such, protests like the die-in are powerful not only because of the ways they allow us to encounter each other, but because of their prophetic material/corporeal disruptions of aesthetic, economic, and political systems that instantiate white, capitalistic, patriarchal power to the neglect, disregard, and exploitation of vulnerable communities. Moreover, the erotic ritual activity of the body informs a kenotic ethical posture that privileges mutuality above hierarchical notions of power. As such, die-ins operate as erotic defiance in that they are grounded in a love for the bodies and beings of Black people,

---

57 Lorde, "Uses of the Erotic," 58–59.

and that they demonstrate this love through a mutuality of shared mission, breath, and flesh. Through prophetic advocacy and experiences of vulnerability, protestors embody solidarity, seek mutuality, and collaborate toward a shared vision, cohering those once estranged in sacred union. Moreover, the communal eroticism of solidarity demonstrates the multiple dimensions of erotic agency, including those beyond individual pleasure.

CONCLUSION

Theorization of the Erotic

As I have worked on this project, I have often been accused of using the term *erotic* as a way to grab the attention of the masses. I am told I am tricking people into believing titillating content awaits—sexual exploits, salacious details, or even access to my body. These expectations and assumptions are in step with historical discourse on the erotic, valuing a woman's body only so far as it may profit or pleasure a man. My accusers are often looking for sensation without the responsibilities that come along with feeling, as Audre Lorde says. They are consenting to the pleasure, but not the fullness of the human that offers such pleasure, even when that human is themselves. Rather than transcending or transforming traditional constructions of the erotic, which by and large are overdetermined by the sexual, these conceptions mimic the rhetoric of erotophobia. Missing is a theological or pneumatological account of the erotic, such that the concept is stunted to a form of individual empowerment, in pursuit of personal aims, with little impact on the community and no consideration for its role in the economy of God.

This investigation of the erotic in the lives of Black women has aimed to theologically account for the power of the erotic that lies in the bodies and being of Black women as more than sexual, or even sensual for that matter, but relational—relational power that has the creative capacity for transformation. Yet, as I watch various artists, authors, and even pop theologians utilize the erotic as a liberative space for Black women, I struggle with the solely sexual register in which it is explored. I fear our preoccupation with proving ourselves human, desirable, powerful, and worthy to a world that doesn't care and perhaps never will has caused us to forget our first love and as such ourselves. Somehow, in an attempt to emancipate Black women from the confines of hegemony's perception of their bodies, Black women's liberation has been diminished to a performance of seeking pleasure, pleasuring ourselves sexually and sharing it with the world.

Attention to the expansive dimensions of the erotic, however, orients us to the many modes of abundant living we are created for and the power for political transformation it makes available. The erotic connects us and therefore reminds us of our responsibility and accountability to one another. Essential to Black women's true liberation is the erotic's role in creating systems of mutuality, wholeness, and transcendence. Looking at three profiles of erotic defiance—acts of care, the performance of sexual agency, and protest—this book has aimed to articulate the role of the body as a resource for moral agency, that is, the means by which individuals can move toward a perceived good, and how bodily agency can be deployed in the work of divine love.

Erotic defiance attempts to reclaim eros as a divine resource for moral agency. Linking erotic phenomena to the capacity of flesh to manifest love for oneself, God, or others, I have expanded on Audre Lorde's assertion of the erotic as the energy for change, arguing that the erotic is a key capacity of Black flesh in the disruption of hegemony and the construction of alternative realities, free of the desecrating powers of racism and sexism. As Lorde theorizes, the erotic connects, enlivens, and inspires women who have "numbed up and dumbed down" to keep their sanity in a world that coerces them into disembodied and disimpassioned existences in the maintenance of male power.[1] Recognizing the disfiguring similarities of racism and sexism, their correlation of raced and sexed bodies with sexual danger, and their mutual strategies of dispossession and disempowerment, I have posited erotic defiance as an appropriate means of disrupting Western hegemony's assault on the bodies of Black women and an effective way of declaring their moral and political agency.

THE BODY

Though Black women's bodies as demonized others bear the brunt of Christianity's discomfort with the flesh, all people, especially Christians, daily

---

1 Lorde, "Uses of the Erotic," 53–59.

wrestle with the idea that the body is a spiritual impediment, begging the question, "What should I do with my body?" Most often this wrestling is quieted by a series of prohibitions of sex, pleasure, and association with the wrong kinds of bodies, with very little instruction on how to embody one's Christian moral agency. Consequently, the body becomes something to negotiate, rather than a gift through which we experience pleasure and create change in the world. Erotic defiance's affirmation of the flesh offers a Christian posture of being in the world that stands in resistance to injustice and domination, and reconciles our relationship with our bodies, presenting them as key resources in bringing about God's kindom.

One of the primary questions of this project has been the relationship between discourse and the body. I have consistently wrestled with the effectiveness of discursive strategies to truly transform our praxis and the status of subordinated and excluded groups in our society. While I agree that discourse is an effective method for challenging hegemonic powers, this project represents my assertion that the manner in which we use our bodies is all the more effective. I make this argument amid contemporary campaigns that assert Black lives matter and Black girls rock and historical campaigns that assert Black is beautiful, while Black people continue to be gunned down in the street by the authorities, Black girls and women have their heads beaten in day after day by men claiming to love them, and people with power use the strategy of distancing themselves from Black identity as a survival mechanism. Seemingly, efforts to change the discourse are choked by the barrage of messages we perceive through our culture's actions and practices to the contrary, which inevitably triumph.

Privileging the activity of bodies as a discourse, I have presented the erotic as a catalyst for transcendence, a movement from one mode of thinking and being to another. Demonstrated through the power of erotic haptic encounters, acts of care, the conjure of seduction, and erotic solidarity, I have attempted to articulate the erotic power of Black women's bodies as a divine resource for Black—with special emphasis on Black women's—moral and political agency. Grounding this assertion in a womanist/feminist rereading, I posit the erotic as a modality of the haptic that creates alternative realities by offering subjects new experiences that contest normative hegemonic claims as valid.

My turn to experience keeps the body central. The experience of one's body in the world and of other bodies and their impact, I have argued, constitutes the haptic—a mode of physical sociality that allows bodies to transform and be transformed by the world. It accounts for the power of material bodies to shape and inform the world and their sensory role in experience, which shapes and informs the identity of the subject. The exercising of erotic modalities of the haptic (i.e., loving touch, celebratory, affirming cultural expression, and collaboration with the Spirit of God) showcases its ability to resuscitate the will and declare the sovereignty of God's order and God's intention of freedom. The free will of humanity is disclosed in our participation in the haptic. It is the human capacity to produce goodness or evil in the world, through the power of the flesh. Thus the erotic, I argue, generates goodness in the world by drawing back together dismembered counterparts like the subject and the body, humanity and the divine, and human beings separated by difference and allows the manifestation of the love of God to orient the construction of knowledge and meaning in the world.

The haptic also underscores the importance of the experience of the body in the work of transformation and the role of erotic encounter in facilitating experiences that move humanity toward empowered, loving relations of mutuality. It is my way of locating instances of encounter, penetration, mutuality, the beginnings of solidarity and therefore the first step toward union. Moreover, I have argued that as Black women shape the experiences of others through their haptic relationality, the importance of gearing those interactions toward the erotic becomes vital to the material liberation of Black women and Black people in the here and now. In addition to offering a new experiential narrative of the flesh, the erotic reinvigorates the will, spurring those who experienced bodily dispossession to moral responsibility through personal and communal accountability, and moves Black subjects from nihilism to moral and political engagement.

The debunking of the demonization of the erotic and its embrace as a resource for agency stunts the power oppressive designations of the erotic have over our personal and political freedoms. It gives us access to the resource inside of us, which gives way to corporeal and relational power and agency, especially among those who are oppressed. As such, erotic defiance at its heart is a moral *and* political strategy for Black liberation. It usurps control from empire's coercive regimes of power, defying and contesting the ideologies of hegemony through the willful rebuke of Western values, including the unapologetic embrace of bodies, sex, and pleasure as an assertion of freedom, autonomy, and self-possession.

Invalidating the superiority of Western aesthetics through willful disregard, erotic defiance reveres that which is coded as inferior, dangerous, and depraved in Western grammar as a way of asserting the beauty and goodness of Black womanhood and asserting their authority over their bodies and being. Accordingly, I have posited erotic defiance as a form of self-love, a deep engagement in and celebration of the subordinated and demonized experiences, perspectives, and cultural meanings of Blackness and Black womanhood. As such, I suggest erotic defiance as a practice of resistance to the dehumanizing, objectifying exploitation and confinement of Black existence. I have argued that the erotic inspires us to resist and can be used as a device of resistance in light of its significance in Western Christian culture. In this way, the erotic and Black self-love represent similar technologies of the embodied self that rely on self-definition and self-formation. Erotic and self-loving postures prove beneficial for Black moral agency, in that they transgress normative expectations of docility by asserting authority and ownership over one's own body and mobilizing the marginalized to action.

All assertions of Black humanity and dignity are inherently protest. All Black moral agency begins with the fight to maintain one's dignity in a society that profits from their disgrace. In this way, Black moral agency is always political. Through haptic practices, organizing principles of particular political rationales are enacted. While erotic care of the soul and erotic conjure are less combative, in that they use less confrontational measures to confront oppressive regimes of power head on, they are no less political. Both assert Black women's somebodiness, their values of self-possession and autonomy as free subjects, exemplifying the erotic as political power and a resource that confronts and resists the deleterious pornographic modes of resistance fomented by greed and a lust for power. Erotic solidarity turns to more explicitly political activities, meaning intentional attempts at communal power through acute clashes and conflict with governing powers, employed by Black women, the Black community, and their allies in the assertion of freedom and the pursuit of justice and the fullness and richness that constitute wholeness.

While pleasure, as I have argued, functions as an epistemology and is an important feature in identity formation and the impulse for resistance, when sexual gratification is our only point of reference for our understanding of erotic power, we fail to see the value of other kinds of human relationality in facilitating such fulfillment. This, I aver, is a distraction from the many modes of abundant living for which humans were created. Moreover, this often self-centered pursuit of pleasure hinders our participation in communal responsibility and the way it contributes to systems of mutuality and wholeness that make us all stronger.

Accordingly, this project contributes to theological discourse on sexual ethics. Many people, especially young people—both churched and unchurched—allow their theologies and ethics of their bodies, particularly their sexual ethics, to be shaped by popular culture. Clarity regarding the intentions of erotic defiance provides insight into the impact womanist/feminist re-readings of the erotic have on Christian ethics. The promotion of a healthy relationship with the erotic serves to encourage future church leaders to move away from the dichotomy of "evil and holy" and engage in teaching that might function to circumvent and challenge media messages with a fuller, healthier approach. Instead of the systematic condemnation of all things sexual, redemption and expansion of the erotic offers the church the opportunity to participate in crafting alternate perspectives that challenge images and ideas that have until recently wreaked havoc upon the psyches of men and women and remained completely unchecked.

Framing the erotic as sacred promotes such a theology and lays the foundation for an ethic of the erotic grounded in love and justice. Moreover, redeeming the erotic promotes a reintegration of the human experience that is both inclusive of the erotic and body affirming, resulting in individuals who are more likely to bring concerns about their bodies, including sexual and erotic concerns and the treatment of others' bodies, on a micro and macro level, to God and to the church, rather than burying them in destructive practices like meaningless relationships and violence against others.

This book's sustained reflection on the relationship between the erotic and the Holy Spirit from a womanist perspective embraces doctrinal Christianity, allowing for a critique of the incoherence of normative Christian ethics to the ethical situations of marginalized communities. From the demonization of Black bodies and the question of how Christians should respond to same-gender loving couples to issues of sexual purity and the myth of Anglo-Saxon election, Christian doctrine about the body matters. What we do with our bodies has creative power. In addition to reproductive power, our bodies construct meaning and generate material and relational consequences in the world, which have lasting significance in the material realm. It is my belief that our corporeality is the principle means by which we participate in divine creativity. From the role of the erotic practices in manifesting a more whole and powerful image of Black womanhood to the sacrifice of erotic solidarity in acts of protest, the body and its manifestations of love for the self and the other in concrete reality change our world.

Accordingly, I argue that all human transformation requires the participation of flesh and blood. All progress demands the erotic activity of material bodies. This book serves as an emphatic plea to Western white Christianity and contemporary feminist and womanist movements to repent of their demonization of the erotic and from relegating the erotic to the sexual and to take up erotic modes of the haptic, specifically erotic defiance as a form of embodied witness to the world of the good news of the body and the freedom and value of all of God's children. For it is only through the power working in and through our flesh that justice and love can reign.

FINAL THOUGHTS

Erotic defiance facilitates alternative experiences of Black flesh—first, for Black people who have been wounded by the stigma of Blackness, and second, for those of other races and cultures whose concept of Blackness has been stunted by Western hegemony. Such experiences operate as more than just traditional representation strategies, but allow Black flesh to contest hegemony's overdetermination of Black identity through experience.

After completing this project, I continue to wrestle with whether erotic relationality has the power for systemic transformation. At the outset of the project I was confident that embodied experiences would and could beget crises of legitimation for those whose exposure to Black women was limited to the discursive. However, racialized violence in the United States has persisted and even taken on new heinous dimensions as seen in the killing of George Floyd and Tyree Nichols. Moreover, the pervasive apathy that accompanies Black death caught on video suggests to me that hegemony colors experience to such a degree that even interpretation of that which we experience is governed by racist, sexist significations. This realization has underscored the importance of intimate relationality among different communities and the power of the erotic to transform. Visual reports from the media are not enough. Firsthand accounts and stories are not enough to call the humanity of "the other" to people's attention. This book has disclosed that only the erotic—that is, embodied, intimate engagement with others through shared pursuits like creative expression, worship, care, and political engagement—can accomplish transformation. The spoken and written word is powerful, but embodied experience with the help of God transforms.

Bibliography

Althaus-Reid, Marcella. *Indecent Theology: Theological Perversions in Sex, Gender and Politics*. New York: Routledge, 2000.

Anderson, Carol. *White Rage: The Unspoken Truth of Our Racial Divide*. New York: Bloomsbury, 2016.

Aristotle. *Nicomachean Ethics*. 2nd ed. Translated by Terence Irwin. Indianapolis: Hackett, 1999.

Athanasius. *On the Incarnation*. Translated by Penelope Lawson. Crestwood, NY: St. Vladimir's Seminary Press, 1998.

Baker-Fletcher, Karen. *Dancing with God: The Trinity from a Womanist Perspective*. St. Louis: Chalice Press, 2006.

Baldwin, James. *The Fire Next Time*. New York: Dial, 1963.

Berry, Daina R. *The Price for Their Pound of Flesh: The Value of the Enslaved from Womb to Grave in the Building of a Nation*. Boston: Beacon, 2017.

Branch, Enobong Hannah. *Opportunity Denied: Limiting Black Women to Devalued Work*. Piscataway, NJ: Rutgers University Press, 2011.

Bush-Baskette, Stephanie R. *Misguided Justice: The War on Drugs and the Incarceration of Black Women*. Bloomington, IN: iUniverse, 2010.

Butler, Lee H. "The Spirit Is Willing but the Flesh Is Weak." In Pinn and Hopkins, *Loving the Body*, 111–20.

Cannon, Katie. *Black Womanist Ethics*. Eugene, OR: Wipf and Stock, 1988.

———. *Katie's Canon: Womanism and the Soul of the Black Community*. New York: Bloomsbury, 1998.

———. "Sexing Black Women: Liberation from the Prisonhouse of Anatomical Authority." In Pinn and Hopkins, *Loving the Body*, 11–30.

Chireau, Yvonne. *Black Magic: Religion and the African American Conjuring Tradition*. Berkeley: University of California Press, 2003.

Coakley, Sarah. *God, Sexuality and the Self: An Essay 'On the Trinity.'* New York: Cambridge University Press, 2013.

Collins, Lisa Gail. "The Art of Loving." In *Women and Religion in the African Diaspora: Knowledge, Power, and Performance*, edited by R. Marie Griffith and Barbara Dianne Savage, 199–221. Baltimore: Johns Hopkins University Press, 2006.

Comaroff, Jean. *Body of Power, Spirit of Resistance: The Culture and History of a South African People*. Chicago: University of Chicago Press, 1985.

Cone, James H. *The Cross and the Lynching Tree*. Maryknoll, NY: Orbis, 2011.

———. *God of the Oppressed*. Maryknoll, NY: Orbis, 1997.

Copeland, M. Shawn. *Enfleshing Freedom: Body, Race and Being*. Minneapolis: Fortress, 2010.

Costen, Melva Wilson. *African American Christian Worship*. Nashville: Abingdon, 1993.

Crawley, Ashon. *Black Pentecostal Breath: The Aesthetics of Possibility*. New York: Fordham University Press, 2016.

Crumpton, Stephanie. *A Womanist Pastoral Theology against Intimate and Cultural Violence*. New York: Palgrave Macmillan, 2014.

Davis, Angela Y. *Blues Legacies and Black Feminism: Gertrude "Ma" Rainey, Bessie Smith and Billie Holiday*. New York: Vintage, 1999.

Day, Keri. *Religious Resistance to Neoliberalism: Womanist and Black Feminist Perspectives*. New York: Palgrave MacMillan, 2016.

De Witte, Marleen. "Touch." *Material Religion: The Journal of Objects, Art and Belief* 7, no. 1 (2011): 148–55.

Douglas, Kelly Brown. *Black Bodies and the Black Church: A Blues Slant*. New York: Palgrave Macmillan, 2012.

———. *Sexuality and the Black Church: A Womanist Perspective*. Maryknoll, NY: Orbis, 1999.

———. *Stand Your Ground: Black Bodies and the Justice of God*. Maryknoll, NY: Orbis, 2015.

———. *What's Faith Got to Do with It? Black Bodies/Christian Souls*. Maryknoll, NY: Orbis, 2005.

Douglas, Mary. *Natural Symbols: Explorations in Cosmology*. 2nd ed. New York: Routledge, 1996.

Du Bois, W. E. B. *The Souls of Black Folk*. New York: Barnes & Noble, 2003.

Duncan, Carol. "From Hattie to Halle: Black Female Bodies and Spectatorship as Ritual in Hollywood Cinema." In *Black Religion and Aesthetics: Religious Thought and Life in Africa and the African Diaspora*, edited by Anthony Pinn, 71–90. New York: Palgrave MacMillian, 2009.

Dusinberre, William. *Strategies for Survival: Recollections of Bondage in Antebellum Virginia*. Charlottesville: University of Virginia Press, 2009.

Fett, Sharla M. *Working Cures: Healing, Health, and Power on Southern Slave Plantations*. Chapel Hill: University of North Carolina Press, 2002.

Floyd-Thomas, Stacey. *Deeper Shades of Purple: Womanism in Religion and Society*. New York: New York University Press, 2006.

———. *Mining the Motherlode: Methods in Womanist Ethics*. Cleveland: Pilgrim, 2006.

Foster, Kimberly. "Wrestling with Respectability in the Age of #BlackLivesMatter." *For Harriett*, October 13, 2015. http://www.forharriet.com/2015/10/wrestling-with-respectability-in-age-of.html#axzz4f0ufsrWp.

Foucault, Michel. *The Archaeology of Knowledge*. New York: Vintage, 1990.

———. *Discipline and Punish: The Birth of the Prison*. New York: Vintage, 1995.

———. *The History of Sexuality*. 3 vols. Translated by Robert Hurley. New York: Vintage, 1990.

Gould, Deborah B. *Moving Politics: Emotion and ACT UP's Fight against AIDS*. Chicago: University of Chicago Press, 2009.

Gray, Biko Mandela. *Black Life Matter: Blackness, Religion and the Subject*. Durham, NC: Duke University Press, 2002.

Gudorf, Christine. *Body, Sex, and Pleasure: Reconstructing Christian Sexual Ethics*. New York: Routledge, 1995.

Guthrie, Robert V. *Even the Rat Was White: A Historical View of Psychology*. Boston: Allyn and Bacon, 2004.

Hall, Stuart. "The Work of Representation." In *Representation: Cultural Practices and Signifying Practices*, 2nd ed., edited by Stuart Hall, Jessica Evans, and Sean Nixon, 11–74. Los Angeles: Sage, 2013.

Harrison, Beverly. "The Power of Anger in the Work of Love: Christian Ethics for Women and Other Strangers." In *Making the Connection: Essays in Feminist Social Ethics*, edited by Carol S. Robb, 3–21. Boston: Beacon, 1985.

Harrison, Renee. *Black Hands, White House: Slave Labor and the Making of America*. Minneapolis: Fortress, 2021.

Harris-Perry, Melissa. *Sister Citizen: Shame and Stereotypes and Black Women in America*. New Haven, CT: Yale University Press, 2013.

Harrod, Howard L. *The Human Center: Moral Agency in the Social World*. Philadelphia: Fortress, 1981.

Heyward, Carter. *Touching Our Strength: The Erotic as Power and the Love of God*. San Francisco: HarperCollins, 1989.

Higginbotham, Evelyn. "African-American Women's History and the Language of the Metalanguage of Race." *Signs* 17, no. 2 (1992): 252–72.

———. *Righteous Discontent: The Women's Movement in the Black Baptist Church, 1880–1920*. London: Harvard University Press, 1997.

Hill Collins, Patricia. *Black Feminist Thought: Knowledge, Consciousness, and the Politics of Empowerment*. New York: Routledge, 2000.

———. *Black Sexual Politics: African Americans, Gender, and the New Racism*. New York: Routledge, 2001.

Hine, Darlene Clarke. "Rape and the Inner Lives of Black Women in the Middle West." In "Common Grounds and Crossroads: Race, Ethnicity, and Class in Women's Lives." Special issue, *Signs* 14, no. 4, "Common Grounds and Crossroads: Race, Ethnicity, and Class in Women's Lives" (Summer 1989): 912–20.

hooks, bell. *Black Looks: Race and Representation*. New York: Routledge, 1992.

Hurston, Zora Neal. *Mules and Men*. Philadelphia: Lippincott, 1935; reprint, New York: Collier, 1970.

Ince, John. *The Politics of Lust*. Vancouver: Pivotal, 2003.

Ingram, Penelope. *The Signifying Body: Toward an Ethics of Sexual and Racial Difference*. Albany: State University of New York Press, 2008.

Irwin, Alexander. *Eros toward the World: Paul Tillich and the Theology of the Erotic*. Minneapolis: Fortress, 1991.

Jacobs, Harriett A. *Incidents in the Life of a Slave Girl: Written By Herself*. Edited by Jean Fagan Yellin. Boston: Thayer & Eldridge, 1861; reprint, Cambridge, MA: Havard University Press, 1987.

Jefferson, Thomas. "Notes on the State of Virginia." In *The Life and Selected Writings of Thomas Jefferson*, edited by Adrienne Koch and William Peden, 173–268. New York: Modern Library, 1998.

Kumari, Ashkana. "'Yoü and I': Identity and the Performance of the Self in Lady Gaga and Beyoncé." *Journal of Popular Culture* 49, no. 2 (2016): 403–16.

Long, Charles H. *Significations: Signs, Symbols, and Images in the Interpretation of Religion*. Aurora, CO: Davies Group, 1995.

Lorde, Audre. "Uses of the Erotic: The Erotic as Power." In *Sister Outsider: Essays and Speeches*, 53–59. Berkeley, CA: Crossing, 1984.

Marcel, Gabriel. *The Philosophy of Existence*. Translated by Manya Harari. Freeport, NY: Books for Libraries, 1969.

Marshall Turman, Eboni. *Toward a Womanist Ethic of Incarnation: Black Bodies, the Black Church, and the Council of Chalcedon*. New York: Palgrave Macmillan, 2013.

Martin, Kameelah. "Conjuring Moments and Other Such Hoodoo: African American Women and Spirit Work." PhD dissertation, Florida State University, 2006.

———. *Conjuring Moments in African American Literature: Women, Spirit Work, and Other Such Hoodoo*. New York: Palgrave, 2012.

———. *Envisioning Feminist Voodoo Aesthetics: African Spirituality in American Cinema*. Lanham, MD: Lexington, 2016.

Merleau-Ponty, Maurice. *Phenomenology of Perception*. Translated by Colin Smith. London: Routledge and Kegan Paul, 1962.

Morrison, Toni. *Beloved*. New York: Vintage, 1987.

Naylor, Gloria. *The Women of Brewster Place*. New York: Penguin, 1982.

Neal, Mark Anthony. *Soul Babies: Black Popular Culture and the Post-Soul Aesthetic*. New York: Routledge, 2002.

O'Brien, M. J. *We Shall Not Be Moved: The Jackson Woolworth's Sit-In and the Movement It Inspired*. Jackson: University of Mississippi Press, 2013.

Perry, Imani. *Prophets of the Hood: Politics and Poetics in Hip-Hop*. Durham, NC: Duke University Press, 2004.

Pinn, Anthony. *Embodiment and the New Shape of Black Theological Thought*. New York: New York University Press, 2010.

———. *Terror and Triumph: The Nature of Black Religion*. Minneapolis: Fortress, 2003.

Pinn, Anthony, and Dwight Hopkins, eds. *Loving the Body: Black Religious Studies and the Erotic*. New York: Palgrave Macmillan, 2004.

Plato. *Timaeus and Critas*. Translated by T. K. Johansen. London: Penguin, 2008.

Porter, Shanette, and Gregory Parks. "Michelle Obama: Redefining Images of Black Women." In *The Obamas and a (Post) Racial America*, edited by Gregory Parks and Matthew Hughey, 116–32. New York: Oxford University Press, 2011.

Riggs, Marcia. *Awake, Arise & Act: A Womanist Call for Black Liberation*. Cleveland: Pilgrim, 1994.

———. *Plenty Good Room: Women versus Male Power in the Black Church*. Cleveland: Pilgrim, 2003.

Ryan, Mike. "Ryan Cooglar Defends His Controversial Scene." *Huffington Post*, July 12, 2013.

Shange, Ntozake. *For Colored Girls Who Have Considered Suicide When the Rainbow Is Enuf*. New York: Scribner, 2010.

Sheppard, Phillis. *Self, Culture, and Others in Womanist Practical Theology*. New York: Palgrave MacMillan, 2011.

Smith, Theophus. *Conjuring Culture: Biblical Formations of Black America*. New York: Oxford University Press, 1994.

Sokolowski, Robert. *Introduction to Phenomenology*. Cambridge: Cambridge University Press, 2000.

———. *Moral Action: A Phenomenological Study*. Bloomington: Indiana University Press, 1985.

Spillers, Hortense. "Mama's Baby, Papa's Maybe: An American Grammar Book." In "Culture and Countermemory: The 'American' Connection." Special edition, *Diacritics* 17, no. 2 (1987): 64–81.

Stephens, Michelle Ann. *Skin Acts: Race, Psychoanalysis, and the Black Male Performer.* Durham, NC: Duke University Press, 2014.

Stubbs, Monya. "Be Healed: A Black Woman's Sermon on Healing through Touch." In Wade Gayles, *My Soul Is a Witness*, 305–13.

Taylor, Keeanga-Yamahtta. *From #Black Lives Matter to Black Liberation.* Chicago: Haymarket, 2016.

Taylor, Mark Lewis. "Bring Noise Conjuring Spirit: Rap as Spiritual Practice." In *Noise and Spirit: The Spiritual Sensibilities of Rap Music*, edited by Anthony Pinn, 107–30. New York: New York University Press, 2003.

Threadcraft, Shatema. *Intimate Justice: The Black Female and the Body Politic.* New York: Oxford University Press, 2016.

Thurman, Howard. *Deep River: An Interpretation of Negro Spirituals.* Whitefish, MT: Literary Licensing, 1945.

Townes, Emilie. *In a Blaze of Glory: Womanist Spirituality as Social Witness.* Nashville: Abingdon, 1995.

———. *Womanist Ethics and the Cultural Production of Evil.* New York: Palgrave Macmillan, 2006.

Turner, Victor. *From Ritual to Theatre: The Human Seriousness of Play.* New York: PAJ Publications, 1982.

Wade Gayles, Gloria, ed. *My Soul Is a Witness: African American Women's Spirituality.* Boston: Beacon Press, 1995.

Walker, Alice. *The Color Purple: A Novel.* New York: Harcourt Brace Jovanovich, 1982.

Walker-Barnes, Chanequa. *Too Heavy a Yoke: Black Women and the Burden of Strength.* Eugene, OR: Cascade, 2014.

Wallace, Mark I. "Early Christian Contempt for the Flesh and the Woman Who Loved Too Much in the Gospel of Luke." In *Embrace of Eros: Bodies, Desires, and Sexuality in Christianity*, edited by M. D. Kamitsuka, 33–49. Minneapolis: Fortress, 2010.

Wardi, Anissa Janine. "A Laying On of Hands: Toni Morrison and the Materiality of Love." *MELUS* 30, no. 3 (2005): 201–18.

Waters, Muddy. "Got My Mojo Working." Written by Preston "Red" Foster. Recorded by Muddy Waters. Chess Records, 1956.

West, Cornel. *Prophesy Deliverance! An Afro American Revolutionary Christianity.* Louisville, KY: Westminster John Knox, 1982.

———. *Race Matters.* Boston: Beacon, 2003.

White, Theresa Renee. "Missy 'Misdemeanor' Elliott and Nicki Minaj Fashionistin' Black Female Sexuality in Hip-Hop Culture—Girl Power or Overpowered?" *Journal of Black Studies* 44, no. 6 (2013): 607–26.

Williams, Delores. *Sisters in the Wilderness: The Challenge of Womanist God-Talk.* Maryknoll, NY: Orbis, 2013.

Wilmore, Gayraud S. *Black Religion and Black Radicalism: An Interpretation of the Religious History of African Americans.* Maryknoll, NY: Orbis, 1998.

Wolcott, Victoria. *Remaking Respectability: African American Women in Interwar Detroit.* Chapel Hill: University of North Carolina Press, 2001.

Index